Cubana

A Caribbean Survivor

BARRY LLOYD

KEY
Books

AIRLINES SERIES, VOLUME 10

Front cover image: Taken during the busier days of Cubana, some of the larger aircraft in the fleet can be seen in this line-up at Havana's José Martí Airport. (Richard Vandervord)

Title page image: An unusual view of a Cubana IL-62 captured while taxiing at Amsterdam's Schiphol Airport. (Michael Prophet)

Contents page image: A scene from the maintenance area at José Martí. (Adr Leo)

Published by Key Books
An imprint of Key Publishing Ltd
PO Box 100
Stamford
Lincs PE9 1XQ

www.keypublishing.com

The right of Barry Lloyd to be identified as the author of this book has been asserted in accordance with the Copyright, Designs and Patents Act 1988 Sections 77 and 78.

Copyright © Barry Lloyd, 2022

ISBN 978 1 80282 472 8

Typeset by SJmagic DESIGN SERVICES, India.

Contents

Introduction

S ince the early 1920s, when the first passenger aircraft began to appear in the Caribbean, many airlines in the region have come and gone. Some were well-known, such as British West Indian Airways (BWIA), Compañía Dominicana de Aviación (Dominicana) and ALM Antillean Airlines, many others less so. Cubana began life in 1929 as a flying club, and, despite a revolution and a period of virtual isolation from the rest of world, it is still flying after 93 years of continuous operation. The aim of this book is to trace the history of the airline, from its modest beginnings through the post-war boom years and the revolution, the result of which was an almost total breakdown in relations with the US and much of the rest of the world. In the late 1950s, the word hijack was introduced into the aviation vocabulary, and Cubana was a victim of many of these events. The combined effects of poor publicity from the hijackings, together with Cuba's isolation from the Western world, had a profound effect upon the carrier's reputation and thus its operation and finances. Additionally, following the revolution, it was forced to turn to the Soviet Union to look for replacement equipment for its ageing fleet. The problems involved in operating Soviet-built aircraft have been well documented, not least the difficulties of obtaining spare parts. Combine this with the restriction of not having a freely convertible currency, and only restricted access to those which are convertible, and the problem is multiplied severalfold. Despite this, Cubana has sought to maintain a presence in the skies outside of Cuba, and its aircraft can still be seen in parts of the region.

The airline has seen it all throughout its many years. During the early years of the 20th century, it was close to the US politically, but then came World War Two, followed by the revolution and the stand-off with the US, which resulted in an embargo, and finally the fall of the Berlin Wall, leading to the demise of the Soviet Union. In 1961, the Cuban government imposed travel restrictions upon its own citizens, hoping to prevent mass migration following the 1959 revolution. On 14 January 2013, the government rescinded the decision, thus requiring Cubans to need only a passport, although the cost of this was equivalent to five months' salary, plus a national ID card in order to travel, and for the first time, they were allowed to take young children with them. More than 180,000 people left Cuba and returned during the first year of the programme.

On 3 July 2009, the Organisation of American States (OAS) finally adopted a resolution to end the ban on membership of the group – a ban that had lasted for 47 years – though Fidel Castro asserted that he was not interested in rejoining. However, the death of Castro in 2011 brought about a thaw in relations with the US, and during the eight years of the Obama administration between 2009 and 2017, significant progress was made in restoring relations. There was a further thaw in 2014, and political prisoners were released, followed by a relaxation of the embargo, reducing import and export restrictions. When President Trump took power in 2017, however, he reversed the policies of the previous administration, thus curtailing any further improvement in relations.

The Cuban government approved a new constitution in 2019. The new constitution states that the Communist Party of Cuba is the only legitimate political party and imposes presidential term limits of five years with no longer than two terms per president. It also recognises private property and strengthens the rights of multinational companies investing in it. Whilst some private businesses have been approved, there seems little possibility of Cubana ever returning to private hands, not least because of its constant indebtedness. It currently needs considerable financial input from the government to keep it operating, not helped by the fact that the national currency, the peso, is not convertible.

The nature of the Spanish language is such that Cubana has had a string of convoluted titles, particularly during the early years of its existence. For simplicity, except where there was a significant name change, the company will be referred to simply as Cubana throughout the book.

Cuba is thought of as one island, but it is actually an archipelago of more than 4,000 islands. The nearest foreign territories are Haiti, 48 miles (77km) to the east, and Jamaica, 87 miles (140km) to the south. Mexico is 130 miles (210km) across the Yucatan Channel, and the US lies 93 miles (150km) across the Florida Straits. Cuba is the largest island in the Caribbean.

Cubana eventually sold this V818 version of the Viscount to Trans Australia Airlines and it is now preserved in Moorabbin Air Museum in Melbourne. (BAE Systems)

Chapter 1

The Birth of Cubana

Aircraft were first seen in the skies of Cuba as early as 1919, when an aircraft was used to take aerial photos of Havana. The founding of Compañía Aérea Cubana (CAC) took place in the same year. The man behind this was Anibal J. de Mesa, a Cuban entrepreneur and millionaire. The company ordered six Farman Goliath aircraft, an ungainly twin-engined biplane built in France, which, like many aircraft of that era, had originally been designed as a bomber. The pilot sat atop the fuselage, in which, typically, 12 wicker seats would be fitted. The aircraft were delivered by sea from France in 1919 and assembled in Cuba. CAC operated flights connecting the major centres of population in Cuba, such as Santiago de Cuba, Santa Clara, Cienfuegos and Camagüey, with Havana. The years following a major world war might not have been the most auspicious timing to launch a new airline, with both local economies and those further afield severely affected by the aftermath, and the airline closed after just 18 months of operation. It was followed by several other companies: Servicio Cubano de Aviación, Líneas Aéreas de Cuba, and Compañía Nacional Cubana de Transporte Aéreo. These operators, all with limited financing, existed somewhat precariously by carrying urgent packages and occasionally wealthy businessmen, both for business and pleasure. None of them existed for very long and were not helped by the Great Depression in 1929.

The next attempt to open an airline in Cuba was born from the ideas of Clement Melville Keys, a Canadian financier. Initially, it was set up in 1929 as a flying school and charter company, with scheduled services beginning in 1930. The company, with its full title of Compañía Nacional Cubana de Aviación Curtiss S.A., was founded on 8 October 1929. The use of the name Curtiss was not a coincidence. Keys was connected to Curtiss via his shareholding in the aircraft manufacturer.

The Curtiss Robin, a high-wing monoplane first built in 1928, was the first aircraft to be operated. There was a small cabin, where two people could sit side-by-side, but the aircraft was used principally to carry passengers and mail on domestic flights.

The Curtiss Robin, one of the early aircraft in the Cubana fleet. This example is preserved at Seattle Museum of Flight. (Visitor7, CC BY-SA 3.0 https://creativecommons.org/licenses/by-sa/3.0, via Wikimedia Commons)

An example of the Sikorsky S.38, used by Cubana on its domestic routes in the 1930s. (EcuRed)

Cuba is a large island, similar in area to Bulgaria or Tennessee, and it was logical, therefore, that air services to connect the larger towns would be the first to be developed. This was done with a Ford Trimotor flying between Havana and Santiago de Cuba, with stops in Clara, Morón and Camagüey. The first of four Trimotors arrived on 4 October 1930, but retained its US registration, NC 8408, throughout its life. On 30 October 1930, Cubana's inaugural flight took place, transporting airmail using the Ford Trimotor, which resulted in Cubana being granted the contract for the carriage of mail within the country in the same year.

The airline also operated the Sikorsky S-38, an American-designed ten-seat amphibious aircraft, the Ford Trimotor and Lockheed L10 Electra. The S-38 began operating in 1931 on the routes to Holguín, with stops in Antilla and Cayo Mambí, all of which are on the coast, the perfect routing for an amphibian, and it operated from the sea at the last two destinations. On 31 January 1932, another flight was inaugurated, this time between Santiago de Cuba and Guantanamo. Later that year, a further new route, operated only on Tuesdays, was opened between Havana and Isla de Pinos, an island to the south of Havana. The island was known as the Isla de Pinos (Isle of Pines) until 1978, when the name was changed to Isla de la Juventud (Isle of Youth). After the revolution, the Cuban government expropriated all foreign-owned property on the island, much of which was owned by Americans, including a Hilton hotel, but it remains very popular with tourists.

Cubana was the first airline in Latin America to operate the Lockheed L10 Electra, a twin-engined low-wing monoplane capable of carrying up to ten passengers. It began operations with the airline in 1935.

A Lockheed L10 Electra sits outside the terminal building in Havana. It carries the original Cuban registration system. (Cubana)

In 1932, Clement Keys decided to withdraw from his aviation interests, which by then included North American Aviation, a holding company for shares in various aviation businesses. It later transpired that he had embezzled funds in order to settle personal debts.

In 1928, Charles Lindbergh flew the Ryan NYP *Spirit of St. Louis* to Cuba, where he was received on 12 February by President Gerardo Machado. Soon afterwards, Pan American Airways System (as it was then called) proposed a purchase of 100 per cent of the shares of the national carrier. Cubana had been experiencing financial difficulties, and the timely Pan American intervention, coinciding with its desire to widen its route network in Latin America and the Caribbean, was of considerable benefit to the carrier. Later, Lindberg inaugurated the Pan American routes from Cuba to South America in the Sikorsky S-42, known as 'The American Clipper'. Cubana was legally acquired by Pan American on 22 March 1932, and on 6 May 1932, once the transfer of shares had been completed, the word 'Curtiss' was removed from the name of the airline. By 1934, the carrier was operating four Ford Trimotors and five L10 Electras. These aircraft were operated on routes from Havana to Camagüey in central Cuba and Baracoa in the far southeast of the island, and also Guantanamo and the Isla de Pinos. The introduction of the L10s made a big difference to the flight times. For example, the flight time from Havana to Santiago de Cuba, a distance of 473 miles (761km), was reduced from 6hrs 15mins to 4hrs 15mins. In honour of this, the service was named 'The Cuban Air Limited'.

Such was the growth in aviation, that in 1935, under the auspices of Cubana, a civil aviation training school was opened in Havana by Ramiro Leonard, who, coming from a family of aviators, was considered to be one of the best pilots of the era. The Ford Trimotors were replaced with seven L10 Electras in 1935, allowing the airline to extend its network to some of the remoter parts of the island.

By 1939, the fleet of Cubana had grown to 12 aircraft. During these years, Cubana's revenue was largely derived from mail carrying. Passenger traffic was limited to business traffic and the very wealthy, but as the economy improved, more people were able to travel, and the fleet grew to match the demand. By the 1940s, further aircraft had been added to the Cubana fleet.

On 24 February 1930, a new airfield was opened near Havana. Known initially as Rancho Boyeros, it was located on flat land in an area to the south of the city. 'Rancho Boyeros' means the 'Bull Drover Ranch', in reference to the name of the plains where the airport was being built. It was known by this name because, many years previously, a local family had built a thatched hut and provided meals and an inn to accommodate the drovers. It was later named Columbia, and finally José Martí, after the Cuban national hero, in recognition of his role in liberating his country from Spain. On 30 October, the first official flight from Havana took place, with the Ford Trimotor carrying mail on the route to Camagüey. Following this, the airport became the principal base of Cubana. On 14 January 1943, the first control tower on the island was opened at José Martí. The government then issued a decree on 8 February 1945, turning over control of civil aviation throughout Cuba from the army to the National Commission for Transportation, and it was 1951 before the first night flight, operated by a DC-3, landed at the airport from Santiago de Cuba.

In September 1933, there was an uprising, known as the Sergeants' Revolt, led by the army, in which the President Gerardo Machado was deposed. The leaders of the revolt, a group of Sergeants, led by Sergeant Fulgencio Batista, would soon have a long-lasting effect on Cuban politics. In 1924, General Machado had been elected president and, following this, opened up the country to tourism, particularly from the US, but this led to an increase in gambling and prostitution and, by extension, corruption. There was a general strike; the Communist party supported Machado, which rang alarm bells in the US, but an army revolt sent Machado into exile in 1933. Following this, there was a military coup, in which Batista took power, although he was not appointed as president at that time. A year

Cubana operated five L10 Electras. (Eddie Coates Collection)

Above: The Ford Trimotor formed an important part of the Cubana fleet. (Cubana)

Left: The same photo, used on the cover of the winter 1931–32 timetable. (Craig Morris Collection)

This copy of the 1948 timetable shows how comprehensive the domestic network was, as well as the early international routes. (Bjorn Larsson/timetableimages.com)

ITINERARIOS

Habana-Camagüey-V. de las Tunas-Manzanillo-Bayamo-Holguín-Stgo. de Cuba-Guantánamo-Antilla-Cayo Mambí-Baracoa

VUELO 482	VUELO 480	VUELO 484	DIARIO	VUELO 481	VUELO 483	VUELO 485
10.30 a.m.	7.30 a.m.	1.55 a.m.	Sal. HABANA Lle.	1.10 p.m.	7.35 p.m.	9.00 p.m.
12.30 p.m.		3.55 a.m.	Lle. CAMAGUEY Sal.		5.25 p.m.	7.00 p.m.
12.50 p.m.		5.00 a.m.	Sal. CAMAGUEY Lle.		5.10 p.m.	6.30 p.m.
1.20 p.m.			Lle. V. DE TUNAS Sal.		4.40 p.m.	
1.30 p.m.			Sal. V. DE TUNAS Lle.		4.30 p.m.	
1.55 p.m.			Lle. MANZANILLO Sal.		4.05 p.m.	
2.05 p.m.			Sal. MANZANILLO Lle.		3.55 p.m.	
2.25 p.m.			Lle. BAYAMO Sal.		3.35 p.m.	
2.35 p.m.			Sal. BAYAMO Lle.		3.25 p.m.	
		5.50 a.m.	Lle. HOLGUIN Sal.			5.40 p.m.
		6.00 a.m.	Sal. HOLGUIN Lle.			5.30 p.m.
3.05 p.m.	10.30 a.m.	6.30 a.m.	Lle. SANTIAGO Sal.	10.25 a.m.	2.55 p.m.	5.00 p.m.
3.25 p.m.	10.50 a.m.	7.00 a.m.	Sal. SANTIAGO Lle.	10.10 a.m.	2.30 p.m.	4.30 p.m.
3.50 p.m.		7.25 a.m.	Lle. GUANTANAMO Sal.	9.40 a.m.		4.05 p.m.
		7.35 a.m.	Sal. GUANTANAMO Lle.	9.30 a.m.		
	11.20 a.m.		Lle. ANTILLA Sal.		2.00 p.m.	
	11.30 a.m.		Sal. ANTILLA Lle.		1.50 p.m.	
	11.35 a.m.		Lle. PRESTON Sal.	9.15 a.m.		
	11.40 a.m.		Sal. PRESTON Lle.	8.16 a.m.		
	11.55 a.m.		Lle. CAYO MAMBI Sal.		1.30 p.m.	
	12.05 p.m.		Sal. CAYO MAMBI Lle.		1.20 p.m.	
	12.35 p.m.	8.05 a.m.	Lle. BARACOA Sal.	8.15 a.m.	12.50 p.m.	

HABANA - VARADERO - SANTA CLARA - CAIBARIEN - MAYAJIGUA

VUELO 488	VUELO 490	DIARIO	VUELO 491	VUELO 489
1.15 p.m.	7.00 a.m.	Sal. HABANA Lle.	9.50 a.m.	5.50 p.m.
	7.30 a.m.	Lle. VARADERO Sal.	9.20 a.m.	
	7.40 a.m.	Sal. VARADERO Lle.	9.13 a.m.	
2.25 p.m.	8.20 a.m.	Lle. STA. CLARA Sal.	8.30 a.m.	4.40 p.m.
2.35 p.m.		Sal. STA. CLARA Lle.		4.30 p.m.
2.55 p.m.		Lle. CAIBARIEN Sal.		4.10 p.m.
3.05 p.m.		Sal. CAIBARIEN Lle.		4.00 p.m.
3.25 p.m.		Sal. MAYAJIGUA Sal.		3.40 p.m.

HABANA-CIENFUEGOS-TRINIDAD-CAMAGUEY

VUELO 498	VUELO 486	DIARIO	VUELO 487	VUELO 499
6.45 p.m.	7.15 a.m.	Sal. HABANA Lle.	12.15 p.m.	12.15 a.m.
	8.15 a.m.	Lle. CIENFUEGOS Sal.	11.15 a.m.	
	8.25 a.m.	Sal. CIENFUEGOS Lle.	11.05 a.m.	
	8.45 a.m.	Lle. TRINIDAD Sal.	10.45 a.m.	
	8.55 a.m.	Sal. TRINIDAD Lle.	10.35 a.m.	
8.45 p.m.	9.35 a.m.	Lle. CAMAGUEY Sal.	9.55 a.m.	10.15 p.m.

HABANA - MIAMI

VUELO 496	VUELO 494	VUELO 492	DIARIO	VUELO 493	VUELO 495	VUELO 497
4.00 p.m.	2.00 p.m.	8.15 a.m.	Sal. HABANA Lle.	11.45 a.m.	5.30 p.m.	7.30 p.m.
5.35 p.m.	3.35 p.m.	9.50 a.m.	Lle. MIAMI Sal.	10.15 a.m.	4.00 p.m.	6.00 p.m.

HABANA-MADRID

VUELOS SEMANALES

Hora Local		DIARIO		Hora Local
Hora Local	9.00 a.m.	Sal. HABANA Lle.	7.30 p.m.	Hora Local
" "	5.30 p.m.	Lle. BERMUDA Sal.	3.00 a.m.	" "
" "	6.30 p.m.	Sal. BERMUDA Lle.	2.00 a.m.	" "
" "	7.00 a.m.	Lle. AZORES Sal.	3.00 p.m.	" "
" "	8.00 a.m.	Sal. AZORES Lle.	2.00 p.m.	" "
" "	3.30 p.m.	Lle. LISBOA Sal.	12.30 p.m.	" "
" "	4.30 p.m.	Sal. LISBOA Lle.	11.00 a.m.	" "
" "	6.30 p.m.	Lle. MADRID Sal.	9.00 a.m.	" "

Hora Standard del Este.

PARA RESERVACIONES EN LA HABANA — LLAME AL A-7241 y M-8171 hasta las 12 de la noche.

later, he took full power, becoming head of the army, and maintained control of the country, albeit by means of a puppet government, for the next 25 years.

Despite the revolt, Pan American did not withdraw its shareholding, and in fact was safeguarded by the revolutionaries, since at that time Pan American was deriving a considerable amount of its revenue from carrying air mail. In 1944, as DC-3s became readily available, Cubana began to replace the Lockheed L10s with DC-3s and later with C-46s. Being a wholly owned subsidiary of Pan American, Cubana's house colours and operation mirrored almost exactly those of its owner, even down to the logo, and the airline's domestic network was designed to feed Pan American's international routes from Havana.

The rapid expansion of Cubana meant that, in 1944, Pan American sold its majority stake in Cubana to private Cuban investors, and on 21 March of that year, the name was changed once again, this time to Compañía Cubana de Aviación S.A., described as a passenger and cargo airline, valued at US$22m, with 796 workers and its head office located at 23 St and O St in the fashionable Vedado district of Havana. It became a mixed company of Cuban private (the majority private shareholder was Fulgencio Batista) and state capital, with a majority of the shares being owned by a bank. This meant that, by 1945, the American carrier held only 42 per cent of Cubana's shares.

With the end of World War Two, DC-3s were plentiful, and the carrier received two such aircraft from Pan American. These were quickly put into service on the domestic routes, serving the principal cities such as Varadero, Cienfuegos, Baracoa and Santiago de Cuba, with daily flights. On 1 May 1945, a daily evening flight between Havana and Camagüey was inaugurated.

On 16 April 1945, Cubana hosted a conference for nations worldwide with developing aviation interests in the famous Hotel Nacional de Cuba (National Hotel) in Havana. As a result of this conference, the International Air Transport Association (IATA), was established, with Cubana becoming a founder member.

Cubana operated ten DC-3s. This one was destroyed during the Bay of Pigs invasion in April 1961. (Eddie Coates Collection)

This 1955 timetable shows the special flights featuring the Tropicana Club. (Bjorn Larsson/timetableimages.com)

CUBANA DE AVIACION

SERVICIOS INTERNACIONALES

MIAMI - VARADERO - HABANA

TABLA TABLE 1	* 463/479 Diario Daily
MIAMI Sal/Lv	5:25
VARADERO Lle/Ar	6:45
VARADERO Sal/Lv	7:05
HABANA Lle/Ar	7:40

Efectivo Dic. 19   Effective Dec. 19

HABANA - VARADERO - MIAMI

TABLA TABLE 2	* 478/462 Diario Daily
HABANA Sal/Lv	2:45
VARADERO Lle/Ar	3:20
VARADERO Sal/Lv	3:40
MIAMI Lle/Ar	5:00

Efectivo Dic. 19   Effective Dec. 19

• Special flight, show on board a round a trip to pleasure to Tropicana Night Club, Havana. Includes full dinner course, drink, champagne, etc. $68.80 all included. Ask your travel agent. ➞

MIAMI - HAVANA

TABLA TABLE 3	☆ 491 Sat Sab Sun Dom Mon Lun	○ 491 Tue Mar Wed Mie Thur Jue Fri Vie	☆ 493 Daily Diario	☆ 497 Tropicana Flight • Daily Diario	☆ 497 Tropicana Special • Thursday Jueves
MIAMI Sal/Lv	7:50	7:50	11:15	7:50	7:50
HABANA Lle/Ar	8:55	8:55	12:20	8:55	8:55

Efectivo Diciembre 16   Effective December 16

HAVANA - MIAMI

TABLA TABLE 4	☆ 492 Sat Sab Sun Com Fri Vie	○ 492 Tue Mar Wed Mie Thur Jue	☆ 496 Daily Diario	○ 498 Mon Lun Tue Mar Wed Mie Thur Jue	☆ 498 Fri Vie Sat Sab Sun Dom
HABANA Sal/Lv	9:30	7:55	5:00	9:30	9:30
MIAMI Lle/Ar	10:35	9:00	6:05	10:35	10:35

Efectivo Diciembre 16   Effective December 16

The Pan American influence is evident in the markings on this DC-3. Note the L10 Electras and Ford Trimotors in the background. (Eddie Coates Collection)

Another view of the standard colour scheme at the time, this one was on CU-T808. (EcuRed)

Chapter 2
Post-war Expansion

An auspicious date in the Cubana Timetable was 15 May 1946, when the airline began its first international route. Inevitably, this was to Miami, using DC-3s. By this time, several more DC-3s had now been acquired. Cubana operated ten of the type in total, which soon enabled a thrice-daily service to be offered to Miami. At this time, the value of the Cuban peso was on a par with the US dollar, and both currencies were in regular use on the island. Cuba had become very popular as a tourist destination, especially with American film stars. Havana had six casinos, horseracing, and nightlife that went on until dawn. In keeping with this, there was also probably one of the earliest examples of an inclusive tour, which featured in the 1955 timetable and was known as 'The Tropicana Flight'. It was an all-inclusive trip, operating from Miami to Havana and combining the flight, hotel and surface transport, together with a visit to the Tropicana nightclub. In 1950, the route had been operated by the DC-3, but such was the demand for seats, that DC-4s soon replaced them on this route.

One of the innovative ideas of Martin Fox, the owner of the famous Tropicana Cabaret, took place on 15 January 1956, when he rented a Super G Constellation, called it the 'Tropicana Special', removed eight seats to provide a free space to serve as a ballroom and arranged an onboard show that

CU-T397 was one of two DC-4s that crashed during its service with Cubana. (R. A. Scholefield Collection)

This C-46, believed to be CU-C202, was formerly operated by Cubana and has appeared in various parts of Havana. Here it is being used as a bar next to Havana's Riviera Hotel.

imitated the Crystal Arches Room, part of the Tropicana Club. The aircraft would leave Havana for Miami on Thursdays at 0800hrs and then take off for the return flight at 2000hrs. During the flight, the passengers were offered a cold Pink Daiquiri (white rum, fresh lime juice, grenadine, superfine granulated sugar, and a slice of lime) to set the mood for what they would receive on a much larger scale at the cabaret. The dance couple, Ana Gloria and Rolando Garcia, would perform their dance show 'Cabaret in the Sky' on board and both danced their mambo routine throughout the aisle of the plane. The plane-hotel-cabaret package cost US$68.80.

In addition to short-haul flights, DC-4s were also used on the Havana–Rome route. From 1948 onwards, the DC-3s were also being used on the route between Havana and Santiago de Cuba and a new route between Havana and the Haitian capital, Port-au-Prince. In addition, the US Postal Union agreed a contract with Cubana to carry mail between the US and Cuba.

With their first international routes now firmly established, the carrier turned its attention to routes further afield. The next obvious choice was Spain, the country that had colonised the island in 1511. For this, Cubana again turned to Pan American, this time to lease, and later buy, DC-4s. The first flight from Havana to Madrid took place on 5 May 1948, on CU-P188 (later CU-T188) *Estrella de Cuba* (*Star of Cuba*). The flight was routed via Bermuda, the Azores and Lisbon, making Cubana one of the earliest Latin American carriers to operate a transatlantic service. On 2 April 1950, the service was extended to Rome. This route was innovative, and thus Cubana became one of the first Latin American airlines to inaugurate a transatlantic route, since few European operators had looked further afield for their operations at that time. The second DC-4, CU-T397, named *Estrella del Oriente* (*Star of the East*) had been received by December 1949. Both aircraft had come from the Pan American fleet.

Carrying its original registration, L-1049E CU-P573 was delivered in 1954. (Eddie Coates Collection)

Numerous inaugural flights took place during 1953. On 15 June 1953, the first of the new Constellation L-049s from Pan-American, CU-T532, was used to inaugurate a service to Madrid, followed by another to Mexico City on 17 September. The following year, on 22 November, Cubana took delivery of one of a larger version, the L-1049E, and registered it as CU-T753. The aircraft had initially been ordered by the Norwegian airline Braathens.

By 1954, the fleet consisted of six DC-3s, three L-049 Constellations, and a C-46 (used for cargo). Three L-1049Gs were also on order. Lockheed provided them with a lease aircraft prior to the delivery of the ordered aircraft and this carried the registration CU-P573, which was normally reserved for private aircraft, presumably because it was on a temporary lease. The aircraft was regularly used on the Mexico City route between 1954 and 1956. It was then returned to Lockheed.

Pan American sold off the remainder of its shares in Cubana in 1954, and the airline became a private company once more. There was no shortage of Cuban investors, attracted by the potential growth of the company, assisted in no small way by the growth of the tourism sector. In fact, during the 1950s, Havana received more tourists than any other Latin American city, with the Havana–Miami route alone operating five flights a day.

Cubana became the first airline in Latin America to operate turboprop aircraft, having ordered three new Vickers Viscounts from the UK, designated as 755Ds. The aircraft were the first operated by

Cubana to be equipped with radar, designed to assist in determining the weather en route – something important in an area that is frequently subjected to tropical storms.

The Viscounts were ordered in early 1956, and the first aircraft, CU-T603, was delivered in May 1956. The remaining two aircraft, CU-T604 and -605, were delivered the following month, but they did not see a long service with the airline, as they were sold to Eagle Airways of Bermuda in 1961. Initially, the aircraft were used to replace the DC-3s on the Miami and Nassau routes, often with a stop in Varadero, and their comfortable pressurised cabins made them very popular with passengers. The Viscounts were also used on the Havana–Port au Prince route and the longer domestic flights to Camagüey and Santiago de Cuba. At the time, the airport at Santiago de Cuba had a somewhat restricted runway, and, following construction of an extension, a Viscount inaugurated the service on 25 May 1956, thus reducing the flight times between the two cities.

In 1958, three further Viscounts, this time the larger 800 Series, were ordered by Cubana. These were fitted with 52 seats and were powered by the uprated Rolls-Royce Dart 525 engines. The aircraft were delivered in 1959 and registered as CU-T621, -622 and -623. CU-T624 had been reserved for a fourth aircraft, but this was never ordered. Somewhat surprisingly, all three aircraft were sold just three years later.

During 1956–57, three further L-1049G Super Constellations, CU-T532, CU-T601 and CU-T602, arrived, although they only remained in service for seven years, following which they were abandoned at Havana, as after the revolution it was difficult to source parts from the US. CU-T601 was converted into a freighter and re-registered as CU-C601 in 1959. These had been ordered new from Lockheed. At this time, Cubana was transporting almost 300,000 passengers per year, of which 50 per cent were on international flights. The 30,000 hours flown during that period were achieved by a fleet made up of three Super G Constellations, one standard Constellation, three Viscounts, six DC-3s, and four Bristol Britannias, which had been acquired between 1958 and 1960.

On 5 March 1956, Cubana began the inaugural service between Havana and Madrid and, on 12 May, opened the Havana–New York route. With the jet about to become significant in worldwide civil aviation, Cubana placed an order on 10 June 1957 for two Boeing 707-121s, with an option on a third. However, neither the order nor the options were taken up, because of the later embargo imposed by the US. Instead, both aircraft went to Western Airways in the US. In December 1957, Cubana bought two DC-4s from Pan American, with a view to opening new routes to Key West and West Palm Beach. Additionally, in May 1957, Cubana ordered four Bristol Britannia 318 series, known at the time as 'The Whispering Giant', straight from the manufacturer, designed specifically

A jokey advertisement aimed at businessmen, promoting Cubana's non-stop flight to New York with the Super Constellation. (Cubana)

The Britannias flew long-haul flights for Cubana. CU-T670 is seen here at Lima, Peru, in 1972 (Alan Scholefield)

Cubana operated four Britannia 318 Series aircraft. This one was delivered in 1958. (Bob O'Brien Collection)

In later years, the Britannias carried the full Cubana colour scheme. (Bob O'Brien Collection)

to Cubana's requirements. The first of these, CU-T668, was delivered in December 1958. The second aircraft, CU-T669, was delivered in 1960. These were bought with the intention of serving New York and Madrid and replacing the DC-4s. In 1959, a Cubana Britannia broke the flight time record between Havana and New York, flying 1,473 miles (2,370kms) in 3hrs and 28mins; at an average speed of 426mph (685kph), setting up a significant challenge to the North American competitor operating on the route, which was still using piston-engined aircraft. The use of the Britannias on the Madrid route also meant that Iberia Airlines was up against stiff competition for the same reason. The Britannia was also used on the Mexico City route. In 1975, the Cubana Britannias were taken off scheduled services and used to transport soldiers of the Cuban Revolutionary Armed Forces to Angola, to take part in Operation *Carlota* as a proxy army for the Soviet Union, supporting troops in the civil war that took place, with interludes, between 1975 and 2002, though the Britannias themselves only served through the mid-1980s. When the US pressured Barbados to refuse landing rights for the flights, the Britannias were fitted with additional fuel tanks in the passenger cabin, enabling them to fly non-stop from Havana to Luanda, Angola, albeit with a reduced passenger load. A modification to enable access to the cargo bay from the cabin was also made.

Arrivals into Luanda were scheduled to take place during the night, with all the lights on the aircraft switched off. Each flight carried a 'heavy' crew, i.e., two sets of pilots, but even so, the pilots often flew beyond their flight-time limits. In total, Cubana's Britannias performed over 100 flights between Cuba and Angola in the 1980s, as part of the operation. By this time, production of the Britannia had long ceased by Bristol, and spare parts were impossible to find. Cubana's Britannias had been built late in the production cycle, and most examples were already out of service by then. Undaunted, Cubana's engineers manufactured them from scratch and occasionally adapted existing parts. One particular example of this was the brake units from the IL-18, which, with a little work, were able to be fitted successfully to the Britannias. The Britannias were in the Cubana fleet for more than 30 years, only being retired in March 1990, with at least one aircraft being operated by Aero Caribbean. In the late 1970s, the major checks on the aircraft took place at Monarch Engineering at Luton Airport.

As the airline continued to grow, it introduced its own inflight magazine, titled *Aeroguía Cubana*, which was first published in March 1954. Such concepts were a rarity at the time, but

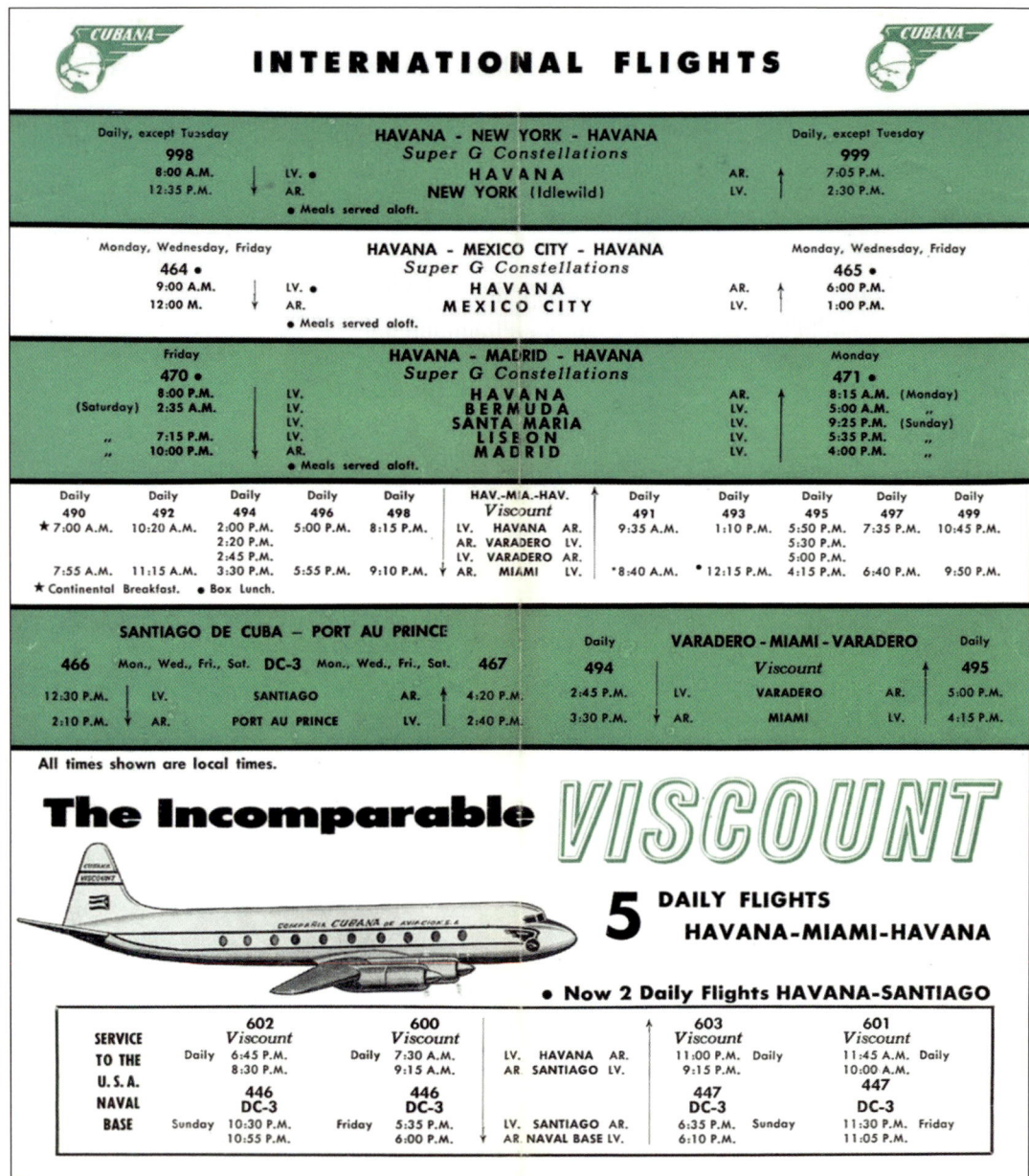

A copy of the Cubana timetable from 1956, showing the routes to New York and Madrid, and advertising the introduction of the Viscount. (Antonio Bordoni collection/timetableimages.com)

the magazine would be printed in Spanish and typically contain about 60 pages, with subjects such as Cuban culture and folklore, and places of entertainment in Havana. The magazine was well supported by local advertisers, such as Bacardi, the Tropicana Night Club and the large department store El Encanto. Additionally, in 1957, to reflect its independence from Pan American, the airline also chose a new logo, the first since its inception, which it considered was more representative of the jet age.

Above: The first of the three Viscount 755s arrives at Santiago de Cuba Airport on an inaugural flight from Havana in May 1956. (Cubana)

Right: Another of the Viscount 755 series supplied new to Cubana during 1956. (Eddie Coates Collection)

Once again, the Pan American influence is apparent on the Viscount as it taxies out at Havana. (Cubana)

Chapter 3

The Revolution

Since politics plays such a pivotal role in the history of Cubana, it is important to recall the events that took place during the lead-up to, and shortly after, the revolution, which in turn had a significant impact on Cubana. For much of its history, the nation of Cuba has been something of a political plaything for the more powerful nations. Beginning with the Spanish occupation in 1511, Cuba was a colony of Spain until the Spanish-American War of 1898, when the US occupied the island nation. It was granted a form of independence in 1902, although it remained a US protectorate. Cuba formally became independent from the US on 20 May 1902, henceforth to be known as the Republic of Cuba. The US, however, retained its right to be involved in the affairs of Cuba, with particular emphasis on its finances and foreign relations. As part of this, the US was to lease the Guantanamo Naval Base from Cuba for an indefinite period. Politically, the US began to take an active interest in the tropical island, which lies just 90 miles (145km) from Key West, the southernmost part of Florida.

The politics of Cuba have always been somewhat complicated. In 1906, full population elections took place, but the results were disputed and there was a short civil war for a few months. The US sent forces to Cuba and reoccupied it, sending a governor to run the country for the next three years. Following this, self-government was eventually restored.

Batista's firm control over Cuba was appreciated initially in the US, not least because there had always been significant communist support from powerful factions within the island, which Batista

CUBANA de AVIACION

ITINERARIOS INTERNACIONALES, EFECTIVO DICIEMBRE 1 DE 1965

HABANA				MEXICO			MADRID		PRAGA		MOSCU			
CU-464	CU-476	OK-524	CU-470	IB-942	SU-048		VUELO NUMERO		SU-047	IB-941	CU-471	OK-523	CU-477	CU-465
Britannia	Britannia	Britannia	Britannia	S. Const.	TU-114		EQUIPO		TU-114	S. Const.	Britannia	Britannia	Britannia	Britannia
F	Y	Y	Y	F/Y	F/Y		CLASE		F/Y	F/Y	Y	Y	Y	F
Lu-Mi-Vi	Ma.	Ju.	Do.	Sa.	Sa.		OPERA		Ju.	Vi.	Mi.	Ma.	Vi.	Lu-Mi-Vi
3:30am	10:00am	10:00am	11:00am	8:00am	7:15am	Sal.	HABANA	Lle.	9:35am	11:50am	5:00am	7:45am	7:30am	5:15pm
10:45am						Lle.	MEXICO	Sal.						1:00pm
- - - -	*6:30pm	*6:35pm	*7:30pm			Lle.	GANDER	Sal.			*11:00pm	*1:20am	*1:30am	- - - -
- - - -	*8:00pm	*8:35pm	*9:00pm			Sal.	GANDER	Lle.			*9:30pm	*11:50pm	*12:00pm	- - - -
						Lle.	SHANNON	Sal.				x 8:25am	*3:30pm	- - - -
- - - -						Sal.	SHANNON	Lle.				x 7:00pm	*7:00pm	- - - -
			Lu. 8:30am	Do. 11:00am		Lle.	MADRID	Sal.			Ju. 10:00pm	Ma. 6:00pm		- - - -
	Mi. 8:30am	Vi. 9:45am	- - - -	- - - -		Lle.	PRAGA	Sal.			- - - -	Lu. 3:40pm	Ju. 4:00pm	- - - -
- - - -	- - - -	- - - -	- - - -	Do. 7:30am	Mi. 10:05pm	Lle.	MOSCU	Sal.	- - - -	- - - -	- - - -	- - - -	- - - -	- - - -

| HORAS LOCALES | (*)—Parada Técnica | (x)—Derecho a tráfico Shannon-Praga-Shannon | F—Clase Primera | Y—Clase Turista | HORAS LOCALES |

Note the changes to the destinations following the revolution, and the inclusion of the Tu-114 service in this 1965 edition of the Cubana timetable. (Björn Larsson/timetableimages.com)

This IL-14 is distinguishable by its unusual nose configuration. It was converted after delivery to Cubana to be an IL-14 FKM (aerial photography version) and later served with Aero Caribbean. (Richard Vandervord)

kept under control. In 1944, Batista left Cuba and went to live in Florida. America now feared that there would be a communist uprising within the country. During his time in office, Batista's support within Cuba came from corrupt politicians and the military. Before coming to power, he had profited from inflated prices in government contracts, together with the proceeds of gambling. He returned to Cuba to run for the presidency in 1952, knowing that he had never been popular as a leader, and that he faced almost certain defeat. He then fomented further unrest by staging another military coup. Once back in power, he received considerable assistance from the US, not least because he immediately took steps to outlaw the Communist Party of Cuba. Despite his authoritarian stance, objections to his form of government began to grow; there were problems with health, housing and employment throughout the country. Having regained power, Batista set about systematically reducing the civil freedoms of Cubans and began to use the lottery and illegal gambling as sources of personal wealth. Corruption also flourished elsewhere in public life. Police corruption grew, and there was censorship of the press and other media outlets. Any form of communism discovered, especially those of political organisations, would be suppressed by the use of violence, torture and even public executions. Such was the level of corruption, something that had been present in Cuba before this time, that even the most desensitised citizen was shocked at how widespread it had become. The public, at this point well aware of what was happening, began to tire of his authoritarian rule. Increasing acts of rebellion began to take place, and by late 1958 it had become a popular form of insurrection. Rebels captured the town of Santa Clara in the centre of the island in 1958, and, under pressure from the US embassy, Batista prepared to flee the country. His first choice was the US, but they refused him, so he looked to Mexico, which also refused him. Finally, he flew to the Dominican Republic on 1 January 1959. It was actually Portugal's dictator, António Salazar, who allowed him to settle there, living first on the island of Madeira and later Estoril, with the proviso that he completely abstain from politics.

The leader of the rebels, Fidel Castro, entered Havana just a week later, returning from his stronghold in the south of the country. The US government, believing that Castro would form a movement to bring democracy to Latin America – many Latin American countries were being led by dictators during this era – initially reacted favourably to the new government. Fidel Castro visited the US on a number of occasions and was invited to give speeches at Harvard University. He was even received by Vice President Richard Nixon during the late 1950s. In the meantime, American tourists continued to flock to Cuba for their vacations.

As one would expect, there had been a lot of conflict between Castro and Batista prior to the takeover, and pro-Batista pilots refused to transport weapons and to fly over the conflict zones in the centre and south of the country, for fear of being shot at. On 9 April 1958, four pro-Batista Cubana pilots hijacked a C-46 and flew it to Florida, where they requested political asylum. Just a few days later, a DC-3 on a regular service between Havana and Santa Clara was hijacked by the pilots, with the same result.

It was then the turn of the pro-Castro rebels to begin the hijackings. On 21 October 1958, a Cubana DC-3 was hijacked with 14 passengers on board, forcing it to land in an area held by rebels. The following month, a Viscount, CU-T603, was hijacked, but for various reasons was unable to land and crashed into the sea, killing most of those on board. A more detailed description of this incident is given later in the book. A number of other attempts were made by supporters of Batista to hijack aircraft to the US, but Cubana was by no means unique in this, with other airlines operating into Cuba having similar experiences.

However, later events, such as the summary execution of Batista's supporters in 1960, plus the appropriation of huge tracts of land following a decree signed by Castro, much of it owned by

Originally delivered to Cubana in 1961, IL-14 CU-T816 eventually became a coffee shop in Santiago de Cuba.

CU-T831 was the subject of a hijacking in March 1966, in which the captain was killed. The aircraft was named in honour of him. More details are in Appendix 1. (EcuRed)

An early version of the AN-24, seen here at Lenin Park, Havana. These aircraft were delivered by sea and assembled in Santiago de Cuba. (Richard Vandervord)

The Antonov 24s were ordered as replacements for the DC-3s on domestic and short-haul routes. (EcuRed)

Americans, quickly soured relations between the two nations. The US responded by imposing a blockade and a range of sanctions, culminating in a total trade ban, and the freezing of Cuban-owned assets in the US. In 1961, the US broke off diplomatic relations, meaning that Americans could no longer travel to Cuba, severely depleting Cuba's vital tourist income, although flights between Cuba and the US continued. However, soon after the revolution, many of Cubana's experienced personnel decided to leave the island, often for the US, thus significantly reducing the airline's skill base. This in turn forced the airline to discontinue all its routes to the US.

Castro's response to the US embargo was to travel to the Soviet Union, where, in February 1960, he signed a commercial and trade agreement with the Soviet Vice Premier, Anastas Mikoyan. Enraged by the thought of Cuba, an island so close to the US mainland, becoming a de facto member of the Soviet Union, President Eisenhower authorised a plan in March 1960 to overthrow the Castro government. An invasion, consisting mainly of Cuban mercenaries based in the US, took place at the Bay of Pigs, an inlet located on the southern coast of Cuba, on 17 April 1961, which resulted in an ignominious defeat for the invaders. However, on 14 April, the CIA, using B-26 bombers, had managed a significant aerial assault, damaging a number of airports and destroying one of Cubana's DC-3s, CU-T138, in the process. The bombing raids also damaged other Cubana aircraft, and, as a result of this, Cubana had to suspend its operations.

In January 1962, as part of the imposed sanctions, Cuba was suspended from the Organisation of American States, which resulted in increased trade sanctions on Cuba. This had the effect of driving Castro further into the arms of the Soviet Union. The Cuban Missile Crisis, which peaked in October 1962, referred to the positioning of Soviet weaponry around the island, bringing the US, Cuba, and the Soviet Union close to war. This plunged relations between Cuba and the US into even greater

Although seen here in Aero Caribbean colours, this aircraft served in a VIP role with Cubana for almost 30 years. (Richard Vandervord)

animosity, with the United Nations warning of the risk of an all-out world war. Fearful of a potential aerial bombardment, similar to that carried out at the time of the Bay of Pigs assault 18 months earlier, Cubana suspended all flights and dispersed its aircraft around the various airports on the island, and the crews of those aircraft that were abroad were instructed not to return. The carrier tried to operate as normally as possible once the crisis was over, and flights were eventually restored, but there was inevitable disruption for a time, and political considerations meant that the route structure of its international flights had to undergo significant changes.

In September 1960, Castro travelled with a delegation to New York for the 15th annual meeting of the United Nations General Assembly. There were a number of acrimonious meetings prior to the main assembly, increasing the fear by the US that his leanings were moving ever closer to communism. Once the main assembly meetings were over, Castro left for Havana but he arrived at Idlewild airport (before it was renamed J. F. Kennedy) instead, discovering that the aircraft he had been using, Cubana Britannia CU-T670, had been impounded, allegedly because of non-payment of debts to American creditors. Castro was furious, but his new friend, First Secretary of the Communist Party of the Soviet Union Nikita Khrushchev, offered Castro one of his own aircraft, an IL-18 in VIP configuration, CCCP-75717, to take him back to Havana. The Cubana Britannia was released the following day, allowing the remainder of the Cuban delegation, many of whom had slept at the airport overnight, to return home.

By now, the die was well and truly cast. Cubana was now left with only ten non-US aircraft – six Viscounts and four Britannias – and these would form the backbone of its operations. Britain had never fully recognised the Cuban embargo – or so it seemed.

Here, in the full Cubana colours, is another example of an early An-24. This aircraft also served with Cubana for more than 30 years. (Richard Vandervord)

Carrying what would appear to be a retro scheme, this An-24 appears to be used for cargo, though there is no cargo door fitted. (Adr Leo)

One of the more recent (March 1985) deliveries of An-24s, this aircraft, called *La Pinta*, underwent modifications in order to compete with the F-27s. (Richard Vandervord)

On 27 October 1964, MV *Magdeburg*, a cargo ship under the East German flag, was leaving the port of Dagenham on the River Thames near London for Havana, when it was involved in a collision with a Japanese cargo vessel, the *Yamashiro Maru*. This was the biggest shipping collision on the River Thames since World War Two. The *Magdeburg* was heading for Havana carrying, amongst other general cargo, 42 British Leyland buses, paid for by Cuba. As a result of the collision, the vessel was badly holed and became beached on a sandbank. Some of the buses were recovered for their spare parts, but most were damaged by the salt water. There was no obvious reason for the accident; visibility was good, and the waters were calm at the time of the collision. Strangely, there was no inquiry into it, and it has long been thought that both the British and US security services were involved. During the mid-1970s, the controversial American newspaper columnist Jack Anderson disclosed that his CIA and also National Security Agency sources had confirmed that the ship collision had been arranged by the CIA with the co-operation of British Intelligence. The bus order was for a total of 1,100 vehicles, a huge order by any standards. With the world of aviation now entering the jet era, this may well have been a warning from the US to Britain not to do any further business with Cuba. The British aviation industry was producing the Comet and the Trident during this time.

One of Castro's first acts when his government took power was to nationalise Cubana. A law was passed on 25 May 1959, through which three smaller privately owned competing carriers were integrated into Cubana. These were as follows: Aerovias Q, which had begun operations in 1946, flying between Havana and Key West using a DC-3; Cuba Aeropostal, which operated four C-46s; and Expreso Aéreo Interamericano, which had begun operations in 1942, also using C-46s. As a result of this, Cubana was given yet another name, this time Empresa Consolidada Cubana de Aviación. The newly nationalised Cubana began operations on 27 June 1961, but earlier, in 1961, Cubana had been

This aircraft also had the same modifications, but crashed into the sea shortly after taking off from Santiago de Cuba. (Richard Vandervord)

This immaculate An-24RV appears to be out of its comfort zone, possibly during a stopover in Canada en route to Cuba. (EcuRed)

CU-T880 was exhibited for a while in Lenin Park, but was finally broken up in 2015.

In March 2003, CU-T1294, while operating a flight from Nueva Gerona to Havana, was hijacked and flown to Key West. The full story is detailed in Appendix 2.

This was the only An-12 in the Cubana fleet. Seen here under darker skies than usual at East Midlands Airport UK, it was collecting an engine from Rolls-Royce. (David Miller)

This immaculate IL-18, CU-T900, operated for Cubana between December 1968 and April 1991. (EcuRed)

The Mil-8 helicopter that was used to convey 36 people to Florida in January 1992. (Joel Whitice via urrib2000)

forced to discontinue all of its US routes, which not only included the profitable routes to Miami and New York, but also those previously operated by the newly integrated airlines, such as Aerovias and Cuba Aeropostal. The impounding of the Britannia that had been used officially to take Castro to the UN was used by the US to indicate its future attitude to Cuba, following Castro's seizure of US business on the island. The cutting off of diplomatic relations in January 1961 was the final nail in the coffin for US routes from Cuba. The Constellations were scrapped during the mid-1960s, once it was clear that there would be no operational support for them.

Cuba's isolation left Cubana with nowhere to turn for new aircraft but the Soviet Union. It now needed long-haul aircraft to replace the Britannias and Constellations, and short-haul aircraft to replace the DC-3s and Viscounts.

Chapter 4

Big Changes 1960–90

Diplomatic events following the 1961 revolution swiftly became a pointer as to how isolated Cuba was about to become. Most damagingly, the US government prohibited the importing of Cuban sugar, Cuba's principal source of income. The countries of Western Europe soon followed, and Cuba was left with the Soviet Union as its sole customer.

It rapidly became clear that fundamental changes in the way Cubana operated would have to take place. Not only would the existing fleet have to change, but also the route network. The Miami and New York routes had already stopped and by 1965, the only long-haul routes were to Madrid, Moscow and Prague. The only destination which had not changed was Mexico City.

Following the signing of the trade agreement with the Soviet Union in 1960, the first of the Soviet-built aircraft, the first of four Ilyushin 14s, a low-wing twin-engined aircraft fitted with 30 seats, was delivered during the mid-1960s. It was soon followed by the IL-18, a four-engine low-wing aircraft capable of carrying 80 passengers. Later, Antonov 12s and 24s joined the fleet. These aircraft were used to replace the DC-3s and DC-4s on their domestic routes, and on other routes within the Caribbean. As a result of this, Cubana became the first airline in the Americas to operate Soviet-built aircraft.

Cubana uses the Mil Mi-8 helicopter as utility aircraft, and they are based all around the island. They are also used to take tourists and ecologists to more remote areas and to Cuba's smaller islands. Cubana

Although this Yak 40 is carrying Aero Caribbean colours, it was previously owned by Cubana. (Richard Vandervord)

CU-T1204 was delivered by sea, and stayed with Cubana throughout its life. (Richard Vandervord)

operated a fleet of An-2 single-engined biplanes, but there was also a huge fleet of An-2s operated by Empresa Nacional de Servicios Aéreos (ENSA), a government-owned operator. ENSA was created in 1995, and its principal maintenance base is in the town of Santa Fé, 12½ miles (20km) west of Havana, but the company has aircraft based all over the country. Although it operates as a separate company, it forms an important part of the overall Cubana operation and works in co-operation with the national carrier. A few aircraft are allocated to each major airfield throughout the island, and also some smaller strips. They are very much utility aircraft that can be adapted for any purpose, but are used primarily for casualty evacuation, crop-spraying and the distribution of mosquito repellent (mosquitoes are very prevalent in Cuba during the rainy season). Some aircraft are also adapted for parachute dropping for sporting clubs. During a period of more than 40 years, almost 200 aircraft were supplied to the island from the Soviet Union, and some still survive.

Politically, it was important that there was a direct link to Moscow, but Cubana no longer had an aircraft with sufficient range to perform this route, even with technical stops, so in 1963 a leasing deal was brokered with Aeroflot, whereby it operated the flight under its own SU prefix, but it appeared in the Cubana timetable. Aeroflot used the Tupolev 114D, a civil airliner based on the Tu-95 bomber, capable of carrying both bombs and missiles. The Tu-114D was adapted especially for this route, the 'D' denoting дальнобойный (dal'noboynyy – the Russian word for long-range), and it was fitted with just 148 passenger seats instead of the normal 200, operating with a higher take-off weight. In fact, in its day, it was the largest and fastest propeller-driven passenger aircraft in the world, with a cruising speed only a little below that of the passenger jets of that era. With such an aircraft, Cubana was able to operate the long-haul flights, typically around 17hrs for Moscow–Havana, making it the longest flight in the world at the time. Initially, the flight to Havana operated via Conakry in Guinea, but after four technical (refuelling) stops had taken place there, the US pressured the Guineans to refuse the flight, on the basis that, with a maximum take-off weight of 171 tonnes, it was too heavy for the runway and parking areas. The route was then amended, so that the flight stopped at Dakar in Senegal. Once again, after four flights, the US accused Aeroflot of using the flights to carry arms, and with its significant political influence in the country, persuaded the Senegal government to refuse any further flights. Algiers was the next technical stop chosen for the route, but this was used only three times before Aeroflot had to completely rethink the routing. Abandoning the flights between Moscow and Havana was not an option, and, after much deliberation, it was decided to operate the flight over the Arctic Ocean. Although promoted as such, the flight was not non-stop, because from Moscow it would then fly the 925 miles (1488km) north to Murmansk in order to refuel (though this is not shown in the timetable) before flying on to Havana. The first weekly flight took place on this route on 7 January 1963, using aircraft CCCP-76480. Only three versions of the Tu-114D were built. Whilst the aircraft could perform its duties adequately, there was an overriding problem with it. So high was the sill of the main passenger door above the ground – approximately 18ft (6m) – that many airports did not have steps tall enough to reach it. In one ignominious episode, when a Tu-114 had been used to fly Soviet President Khrushchev to the US, the aircraft arrived at Andrews Air Force Base, only for the ground handling unit to discover that there were no suitable steps available, and Khrushchev and his entourage were forced to leave the aircraft using a set of makeshift ladders in order to reach the normal aircraft steps. Later, the flights to Cuba were undertaken by IL-62s, and this is covered in the next chapter.

As discussed, Cubana's routes to the US were embargoed in 1962, but, in the meantime, the carrier had begun a new service to Prague, an extension of its Madrid service, using the Bristol Britannias. This route was a stretch, even for the Cubana Britannias, which had been fitted with additional fuel

A busy scene at Havana's Jose Marti Airport, with IL-62M CU-T2159. (Richard Vandervord)

Cubana had a number of different colour schemes. This anonymous IL-62 displays one of the lesser-known examples. (EcuRed)

tanks, and, given that it had to avoid US airspace, the route was flown via Bermuda and The Azores. The routing via Bermuda, which had been in operation since 1948, was cancelled in 1961, following US pressure. In order that they could operate a reciprocal service, Cubana regularly leased a Britannia to Czechoslovak Airlines (CSA). The routing, which began in February 1962, was, however, slightly different initially. The route operated by CSA was via Manchester and Prestwick, but this was later changed to Prague–Shannon–Gander–Havana. Despite similar pressure on Ireland and Canada, both Shannon and Gander, respectively, continued to be used as technical stops by the airline. The Gander stopover could be something of a challenge, with potentially difficult weather conditions in the winter, and the enticement to the crews to abandon their aircraft and seek refuge in the nearby US.

By March 1970, Cubana was employing almost 2,000 people. The fleet at that time comprised ten IL-14s, four Britannia series 318s, five An-24Bs, four DC-3s, four IL-18s, two DC-6s and one DC-4. The carrier was operating regular services, some to countries with socialist leanings, such as Peru, Chile, and Guyana. Panama and various Caribbean destinations were also added to the schedule. It was during the mid-1970s that Cubana moved into the jet age, having received Tu-154s, Yak 40s and 42s, and IL-76s to deal with the requirement for cargo flights. This allowed the carrier to open services to new destinations in South America. Since Canada was not involved in the embargo placed upon Cuba, flights to Canadian destinations began, principally to bring tourists to Cuba. As with the South American destinations, in the mid-1970s, Cubana also began to serve destinations in Africa that were sympathetic to the Cuban doctrine, such as Angola, Cabo Verde and Guinea-Bissau.

The clean elegant lines of the IL-62 are evident in this photo. (Richard Vandervord)

Taken during a rare visit to Heathrow, CU-T1280 was sold to North Korea in July 2012 but later broken up for parts. (Richard Vandervord)

CU-T1225, seen here at Manchester Airport, was the subject of a diplomatic incident. (Ken Fielding)

Cubana's first IL-62 arrived in 1973 on a short-term lease from Aeroflot. Further aircraft arrived in 1974, but four of these were returned to Russia in order to have additional fuel tanks and improved avionics fitted. The primary reason for this was to allow Cubana to fly to Angola, where Cuban revolutionaries were taking part in the civil war there. However, it was still necessary for the IL-62s to refuel in Zaïre. The IL-62s were also used to operate scheduled services from Havana to Madrid, Tripoli and Baghdad and on the route to Montreal. The Havana–Luanda operation became a scheduled service, operating with a technical (refuelling) stop in Sal, Cape Verde Islands. In June 1982, the Cubana service to Luanda operated primarily as Cuban government support for Angola's Communist People's Movement for the Liberation of Angola (MPLA) rebels. The service then continued to Maputo, Mozambique's capital. Cubana subsequently leased one of its IL-62s to Angola's national airline, TAAG, in order that it could also operate flights between Luanda and Havana, thereby supplementing the Cubana operation, and allowing the African carrier to operate its first transatlantic route.

On 8 January 1973, Cubana began operating the IL-62s to Santiago de Chile via Lima. However, following the overthrow of President Salvador Allende, the first Marxist president in South America to be democratically elected, and his subsequent death on 11 September that year, the service was suspended. A co-operation agreement with the East German airline Interflug meant that a new route between Havana and East Berlin was inaugurated on 3 April 1973, thus establishing Interflug's first scheduled transatlantic service. Cubana also began its first route to Iraq in the late 1970s, but the route was discontinued in the early 1980s.

Despite the continuing US embargo, in 1978, the Carter administration took the decision to open a 'Special Interests Section' building in Havana. This was not a formal diplomatic representation in the way that an embassy is, and such an arrangement is only possible when both countries do not share diplomatic relations but have a formal diplomatic agreement. It was nevertheless a significant

CU-T1252 takes a break between flights. Note the retractable tail support wheel, which was a standard fit. (Bob O'Brien)

Despite its immaculate condition in this photograph, CU-T1282 only served 14 years with Cubana. (Richard Vandervord)

AN AIRBORNE DIPLOMATIC INCIDENT

On 9 April 1982, the Brazilian Air Force became aware of a large aircraft in its airspace for which they had no flight plan. It quickly became apparent that the aircraft was an IL-62M, belonging to Cubana. It was CU-T1225. At the time it was traced, it was about 186 miles (300km) north of Brasília, the capital. Several attempts were made to contact the aircraft by the First Integrated Center for Air Defense and Air Traffic Control (CINDACTA 1), and eventually the crew simply responded by saying that they were en route to Ezeiza, the main international airport for Buenos Aires. By now, the Brazilians were becoming quite suspicious, and immediately scrambled two Dassault F-103E Mirage fighters from the nearby Anápolis Air Base. Under the guidance of CINDACTA 1, the pilots located the aircraft, and despite there being heavy thunderstorms in the area, the Mirages climbed above the clouds and increased their speed from Mach 0.98 to Mach 1.15, while they both prepared their air-to-air missiles and positioned themselves close to the aircraft. At this point, the Mirages were ordered to make themselves visible to the airliner, with the leader moving to the left and the wingman to the right of the Ilyushin, until they were very close to the cockpit. A message was broadcast over the radio in English from CINDACTA 1 to the crew of the Ilyushin, ordering it to land immediately in Brasilia. 'Cubana 1225, you have been intercepted! There are two fighters alongside your aircraft. You are ordered to land in Brasília immediately!' After several moments, the IL-62 pilot answered: 'Roger, Roger, Brasília! Give me instructions!' Following these instructions, and with the Mirages still shadowing the aircraft, it eventually landed in Brasilia at 2212hrs.

Once landed, Brazilian troops arrived and began to surround the aircraft. Much to the surprise of the Brazilians, they discovered that there were only three passengers on board: a Cuban diplomat (in fact, the Cuban Ambassador to Argentina) by the name of Emilio Aragonés Navarro, his wife and a boy, the couple's grandson. When asked about the flight, he declared that it was heading for Argentina, but initially, no reason was given for the flight, or the secrecy surrounding it. The aircraft, crew and passengers were kept on the ground for six hours, while the Brazilian and Argentine authorities negotiated over their release. At the time, Brazil had no diplomatic relations with Cuba. Finally, after the aircraft was allowed to continue to Buenos Aires, and the reason for the secret flight was revealed. The Falklands (Malvinas) war was in progress, and the Cuban diplomat simply wanted to arrive in Buenos Aires to begin mediations before his American counterpart and did not want to alert the authorities to their plan. Emilio Aragonés Navarro retired the following year.

presence, and it allowed Cubana to operate charter flights to Miami on a regular basis. However, this arrangement did not last for long, being rescinded by the Reagan administration in 1981. The method of moving staff to and from the Special Interests Section was undertaken by an American carrier, though the operation was denied officially, operated during the night and never appeared in any timetable.

In order to replace the remaining Viscounts and Britannias, Cubana ordered four Tu-154Bs, to be delivered in the early 1980s. These, unsurprisingly, were to be used on routes to countries that were sympathetic to Cuba, such as Nicaragua, Mexico, and Suriname. They were also used for the scheduled services to Canada. Cuba had become particularly popular with Canadian visitors in the mid-1970s, but with only Soviet-era aircraft to operate the services, in 1976 Cubana decided to lease three

DC-8-43s from Air Canada to carry out the operation. Since diplomatic relations between Canada and Cuba were not subject to the embargo, and the aircraft were fitted with Rolls-Royce engines, there were few obstacles to the operation. Additionally, they were used for other flights within the Caribbean and also Guyana.

On 30 January 1981, Cubana began a Havana–Santiago de Cuba–Grenada service using its An-26s. This was largely to support Cuban workers who had been drafted in to build a new airport on the island of Grenada. The airport had been approved to replace the small and totally obsolete Pearls Airport on the north coast of the island, thus allowing larger aircraft to land and, as a result, improve the tourist potential. However, US President Ronald Reagan did not see things quite the same way, convinced that it would be used as a refuelling point for Soviet military aircraft en route to Cuba. The fact that it was being built, in part, by Cuban workers, was enough to convince him that his theory was correct. This was despite the fact that the airport had been designed by a Canadian company, and the specialised work was being carried out by European contractors. Two private American construction companies were also participating in the project. Furthermore, the fuel tanks were clearly visible above ground, something not normally found on a military airfield.

Reagan's pleas to Grenada to stop the building of the new airport fell on deaf ears, however, and, in the early morning of 25 October 1983, units of the US army parachuted onto the unfinished airfield, citing a perceived threat to 600 US students studying at a nearby university. In an ironic twist, the airport was finally completed with a US$19m assistance loan provided by the US and opened to commercial traffic in October 1984. Cubana continued to operate into the new airport.

In 1986, four YAK-42D aircraft were incorporated into the fleet. These aircraft covered domestic routes, routes in the Caribbean and some routes to Central America, post-embargo.

In 1986, Buenos Aires and Zürich were added to the network. A year later, flights to Moscow (by IL-62), Bissau (Guinea-Bissau) via Sal (Cape Verde), and Port of Spain (Trinidad) were inaugurated. Flights to Milan and Cologne were inaugurated in 1987.

CU-T1218 is taxiing out at a busy Orly Airport. (Gerry Manning)

Cubana seemed to like experimenting with different colours and logos. CU-T1256 shows a different font for the Cubana title (Richard Vandervord)

CU-T1265 carries the more conventional colour scheme. The aircraft ended its life in Russia as RA-85721. (Richard Vandervord)

Yet another adaption of the colour scheme. Sadly, this aircraft, CU-T1264, crashed on take-off from Quito, Ecuador. Full details are shown in Appendix 1. (EcuRed)

Cubana operated nine TU-154s. This aircraft spent its entire life – about 25 years – with Cubana. (Richard Vandervord)

The aircraft that Cubana operated invariably looked in good condition. CU-T1253 taxies out at Havana's Jose Marti airport. (Richard Vandervord)

Shannon was a popular stopover point for Cubana's aircraft. CU-T1283 calls in for fuel before crossing the Atlantic. (Malcolm Nason)

This aircraft served with Cubana for nine years before being written off following an accident in Mexico City on 14 February 1991. (Richard Vandervord)

This Tu-154B, CU-T1265, carried several colour schemes during its lifetime, including those of Aeroflot, Hemus Airlines of Bulgaria, and Albanian Airlines. (Malcolm Nason)

Looking a little the worse for wear, CU-T1275 is seen at Shannon, before being flown to Samara (Russia) for a lease with Samara Airlines while still carrying its Cuban registration. (Malcolm Nason)

For a brief period, this aircraft was re-registered as CU-C1222 in Oct 1999. (Richard Vandervord)

CU-T1227 seen during happier days. The aircraft crashed on approach to Mexico City on 14 September 1991. The full details are in Appendix 1. (Richard Vandervord)

The IL-76 is an impressive beast. Cubana operated four of them. (Richard Vandervord)

Same aircraft – different day. After leaving service with Cubana, this particular aircraft was offered for sale by another operator on the internet for US$1.7m in July 2005. (Richard Vandervord)

Cubana operated three DC-8-43s leased from Air Canada. The fact that they were fitted with Rolls-Royce Conway engines meant that they were not subject to the embargo. This was the only aircraft that survived, after the other two crashed in 1976. Full details in Appendix 1. (Malcolm Nason)

Above: This Yak-40 sports yet another version of the Cubana colour scheme.

Left: The monument erected to the victims of the sabotage of flight CU 455. Full details are in Appendix 1. (BCF, CC BY 1.0 https://creativecommons.org/licenses/by/1.0, via Wikimedia Commons)

Chapter 5

The Collapse of the Soviet Union 1990–2000

The collapse of the Soviet Union was as unforeseen as it was unsettling, both for Cuba and Cubana. By this time, in March 1990, Cubana had all its eggs in the Soviet Union basket where aircraft were concerned, operating a large fleet of An-24RVs, An-26s, IL-18s, IL-62Ms, IL-76Ds, Tu-154s, and Yak-40s. These aircraft were covering routes to the Caribbean (Barbados and Kingston) and South America (Buenos Aires, Georgetown, Guyana, Lima, Peru, Managua [Nicaragua's capital], Mexico City and Panama City). In Africa, Luanda in Angola and Bissau, the capital city of Guinea Bissau, were still part of the route network, and a route to Montreal was the sole destination in North America. In Europe, Basle, Berlin, Madrid, Paris and Prague had scheduled flights. At least seven major cities within Cuba were also receiving a regular service.

The Soviet withdrawal from Cuba began in September 1991. This became known within Cuba as 'The Special Period'. It was a trying time for Fidel Castro, with the country experiencing a severe economic downturn. The Soviet subsidies, amounting to between US$4bn and $6bn a year, quickly disappeared, plunging Cuba into a deep economic depression with significant food and fuel shortages, resulting in open protests. The biggest impact was the loss of almost all the petroleum Cuba had

Although in Cubana colours, this Yak-42D appears to have been a lease aircraft. It had previously operated for Aero Asia International, based in Karachi. It had been delivered in 2001 and returned to Russia in 2005. (Malcolm Nason)

The lack of colour scheme in this Yak-42D is probably explained by the fact that it was leased between October 2005 to October 2008 from Russian operator Avia Karat. (Malcolm Nason)

imported from the former Soviet Union. Previously, Cuba had been exporting any oil it didn't consume to other nations, with profits going to the government. In fact, petroleum was the second largest export (after sugar) from Cuba before 1990.

Unhappy with that situation, the newly formed Russian Federation made it clear that it would no longer supply petroleum products on the previous basis, which resulted in a 20 per cent decrease in consumption within two years. Since Cuba is entirely dependent on fossil fuels to run its industries, it had a very dramatic effect on all aspects of life on the island. Offers of food were made by the US, but these were refused by Castro. During the following four-year period, Cuba's gross domestic product – the value of goods produced and services provided in a country during one year – declined by 35 per cent. Cubana had to deal with all these problems at once, while the American embargo continued. The short-term challenge was to keep the existing fleet operational, but with an eye to the future as well.

The effects of the changes on Cubana were devastating. With the economy going quickly into free fall, the airline's income on both domestic and international routes was significantly reduced, but the biggest problem the carrier now faced was keeping its fleet airworthy. Under a so-called command economy, one in which central government controls the level of production, together with the prices that can be charged for the goods produced, the capacity for manufacturing anything in excess of what has been approved by the government, such as additional spare parts and other support equipment, is very limited. This means that, in many cases, the equipment can no longer function until replacement supplies are received, which can sometimes take months rather than days. This is a problem in any business, but absolutely devastating in aviation. Thus, some of the IL-62s, which had been delivered in batches since the late 1970s, were being taken out of service in order to provide spare parts for the newer aircraft. Although Aeroflot had a huge fleet of the aircraft, it was doing the same thing, and was reluctant to release any spares from its own stock.

The one piece of good news in all this was that Cuba itself was becoming an increasingly significant tourist destination, with 2.7 million tourists visiting the island during 2011. Of these, many of whom were primarily from Canada and Argentina, Cubana carried about one third. However, this was not necessarily all good news for Cubana. With a fleet that was becoming increasingly challenging to maintain, coupled with Western consumers' antipathy towards Soviet-built aircraft, the company was lacking the potential to acquire much-needed foreign revenue from Europe and Canada, despite the fact it was citizens from those nations that wanted to visit the island. In general, the airline could barely maintain its domestic and international schedules, let alone provide aircraft to operate holiday charters.

With this in mind, Cubana undertook a fleet renewal process, and in April 2006, confirmed orders for two further IL-96-300s, and three Tu-204s, to cover the longer-haul routes. One of the Tu-204s was to be a cargo version. The aircraft were delivered to Cubana during June and August 2007. At the MAKS Air show in Moscow during the same year, Cubana then signed a memorandum of understanding – a document which, in effect, precedes an official order, but is not legally binding – for the purchase of two more Tu-204s and three Antonov 158s. During these contract negotiations, the cargo version of the Tu-204 was cancelled.

Cubana took delivery of the first three An-158s in April, July and August of 2013, with the second batch following in April and July of 2014, and the final aircraft arrived in April 2015. These aircraft had been ordered to enable the carrier to phase out the An-24s, which had been used on their domestic routes and some of the shorter services around the Caribbean.

In 2008, Cubana also ordered three IL-96-400s, to be fitted with 350 seats, although few of this variant were ever completed, and it is believed that Ilyushin may now be looking at a twin-engined version. A Boeing 767-300ER belonging to EuroAtlantic Airways, carrying the registration S9-DBY, was chartered briefly from February to September in 2009, presumably to cope with the additional traffic for the peak period.

Another leased Yak-42D. This one was re-registered as CU-T1709 in October 2008 and was flown to Ukraine in August 2012 as UR-CKO. (EcuRed)

Cubana occasionally named its aircraft. This Yak 42D, CU-T1277 carries the name *Santiago de Cuba* in small letters on the nose. (Richard Vandervord)

This aircraft, although carrying the full Cubana colours, is believed to have been leased from Tatarstan. (Richard Vandervord)

The possibility to lease Western-built aircraft existed, though the choices were very limited, because most Western-built aircraft carry at least some US-manufactured equipment. A drastic fleet change of any kind also requires a significant amount of re-equipping and retraining, especially for flight crews and engineers. Financing resources were very limited, and the US embargo, coupled with a lack of Western financing and Cuba's own poor financial situation, meant that there was no option, in the short term at least, but to keep the Soviet-built aircraft in service. The last three IL-62Ms, the latest model available, had been received by Cubana in late 1990. Cubana managed to keep these flying for a decade, even after IL-62 production had ceased in the mid-1990s. One solution to the problem was for Cubana to turn to leasing Airbus and Boeing aircraft, using third parties. This allowed them to maintain their services to Europe and Canada, together with the more important Latin American destinations it had served. The situation did not prevent the carrier from serving more than 35 cities around the world, and the last IL-62M in regular scheduled service was retired in 2011.

With a view to improving the overall status of the airline, Cubana entered into a leasing-only agreement with Air France in May 2014. The agreement was designed to cover crew training, technical improvements, management and IT staff. In the same year, the airline began services to Costa Rica, using the An-158s, whilst announcing that it would add a second weekly service to the Mexican resort of Cancun. The island of Puerto Rico was added to the timetable in 2015, also using a leased A319.

In March 2016, Cubana began a new service between Holguin and Santo Domingo using A319s and A320s leased from various different leasing companies. This was also the year in which, for the first time, Cuba received more than four million tourists. Long-haul routes were not forgotten either, with an A340-313, EC-MFB, being leased from Spanish charter operator Plus Ultra Lineas Aéreas for a short period from October 2019.

Seen here with the engines removed, this aircraft crashed whilst on a flight between Havana and Caracas, Venezuela, on 25 December 1999, when it had to divert to Valencia. Full details in Appendix 1. (Richard Vandervord)

Yak 42D CU-T1707, in a very basic colour scheme, takes off from Caracas Airport. (EcuRed)

In the early years of the millennium, the airline was employing more than 5,500 people, but the turmoil in the former Soviet Republics had exacerbated the problem of obtaining spare parts for its Soviet-built aircraft. Nevertheless, Cubana began a significant route expansion. The IL-18s continued to be used on domestic and short-haul services, while the IL-62s were used for the longer hauls to Europe and South America. In recent years, however, the carrier's financial burdens had mounted, resulting in cash shortages. Cubana ran into difficult times as a result of the political and economic difficulties in Russia and Venezuela, the two cash cows upon which the carrier relied for its expansion. The airline had struggled to meet rental obligations for jets and to repay credits issued earlier to renew ground infrastructure.

Despite the challenges of keeping the Soviet-era fleet operational, Cubana continued to operate, but the US continued its antipathy towards the carrier. In the 1990s, the US prohibited overflights by the carrier, despite the fact that Cubana could not fly into the US anyway, although US carriers were allowed to overfly Cuba every day on their routes to Latin America and other Caribbean destinations. The biggest problem caused by the US overflight ban was that of Cubana's flights to Canada. A significant amount of tourist traffic had built up, particularly among those Canadians who wished to escape their country's harsh winters for a warmer destination in the Caribbean. As a result, Cubana launched a complaint to the International Civil Air Organisation, and whilst this was being debated, installed improved navigation equipment on the aircraft operating on the Canadian routes, enabling them to fly over water between the two destinations, thus avoiding US airspace. This, coupled with the enforced detour, put additional financial strains on Cubana at a time when it was already facing difficulties on many fronts.

The rapid increase in tourism meant that it was impossible to increase the fleet fast enough to cope with it, and Cubana found an operator that could facilitate its longer-haul routes within Latin America to Buenos Aires and Santiago de Chile and those to Europe in the shape of Air Outré Mer (AOM), a company nominally based in the French overseas department of Reunion. A DC-10-30, F-ODLX, began operations in October 1991 and operated until March 1992; the European and Canadian winters forming the high season in Cuba. This was replaced by F-GNEM between November 1992 and July 1993. In total, Cubana leased three DC-10-30s, and, by 1992, in addition to the Latin American destinations, the aircraft were also serving various destinations in Europe, such as Paris and Madrid. Fate was to play a hand in this arrangement, however, when, on 21 December 1999, an AOM DC-10-30, F-GTDI, was written off whilst operating Cubana flight CU 1216 from Havana to Guatemala City. The La Aurora airport at Guatemala City is 4,951ft (1,509m) above sea level and can suffer with low cloud. The DC-10 overran the runway after landing in wet conditions, went down a steep slope at the end of the runway, and crashed into 10 houses beyond.

The IL-62s continued to fly to Madrid on the days when one of the DC-10s was not operating, and were also scheduled to destinations such as Basle, Berlin and Brussels, together with Moscow. The Tu-154s were used on the longer-haul Americas services, for example those to Mexico City and Montreal.

In March 1990, Cubana had 5,658 employees and its fleet consisted of 12 An-24RVs, 20 An-26s, four IL-18s, 11 IL-62Ms, two IL-76Ds, eight Tu-154s (five 154B-2s and three 154Ms) and 12 Yak- 40s (with the first example arriving in 1976). Later in 1990, Cubana acquired five Yak-42s (CU-T1242 to -1246), and an IL-76 (CU-T1258) was integrated into the cargo fleet. Over the following decade, Cubana ordered three more Yak-42s: CU-T1272, -1285 and -1708. Cubana's limited financial resources made it difficult to persuade the traditional western financiers and leasing companies to offer finance with

Cubana took delivery of eight F-27s during 1994, mainly to replace the ageing An-24s. (Richard Vandervord)

This aircraft was only in the fleet for seven years, before being sold on to Myanmar Airways (Burma). (Richard Vandervord)

Note the cargo door on this F-27-400, the only one that Cubana operated. The remainder were -600 Series. (Richard Vandervord)

which to buy western-built aircraft. This, together with the US embargo, meant that Cubana's options were very limited, and the company once again turned to Ilyushin and Antonov to renew the fleet.

With even the newer of the An-24s heading towards 20 years of age, and spares becoming increasingly difficult to source, Cubana decided once again to look elsewhere for replacements. In the mid-1990s, it discovered that Aviaco, a Spanish domestic scheduled passenger airline set up by the government at the end of World War Two to supplement domestic demand, was soon to be taken over completely by Iberia and had a large fleet of F-27s available. Cubana bought eight of them in 1994, with seven being the -600 series and one a -400. All were combi versions and were used on domestic services. Because of their age, the F-27s did not see long service and were withdrawn by the early 2000s, with some being scrapped and others being sold on. By this time, many of the aircraft were more than 30 years old. Additionally, a number of ATR-42 aircraft were brought in to serve the regional routes, some of which were transferred to Aero Caribbean.

In the mid-1990s, the airline also set about refurbishing several of its IL-62s, so that the international routes could be maintained (these aircraft were withdrawn from service in 2011). Also at that time, Cubana began to lease aircraft from charter operators, to cope with the growing tourist demand. Once again, the US raised objections to the flights, threatening the operators with the cancellation of US landing rights. The French government intervened and was able to prevent any further action. Such pressures are unprecedented in the history of commercial aviation, but form part of the unrelenting efforts by the US to damage Cubana.

The mid-1990s had seen a rapid growth in the tourism sector, and the second half of this decade continued to be a time of significant expansion for Cubana, with new routes opened to other areas of the Caribbean, including the Cayman Islands, Montego Bay and the French islands of Guadeloupe and Martinique. These were operated by the aforementioned F-27s, which had replaced the An-24s that had been largely taken out of service. The DC-10 routes were expanded to include Frankfurt, Lisbon and Rome. A route to London was opened in April 1997. Cubana also operated a fifth freedom route between Moscow and Las Palmas (a fifth freedom route, put simply, is between two countries other than those to which the airline belongs).

CU-C1257 was originally delivered as a passenger version and later converted to cargo. It now resides in the town of Santa Clara. The Antonov 24RV is believed to be in use as a restaurant. (oldjets.net)

Chapter 6
2000 to the Present Day

The Cuban government was able to lease four ATR 42-300s from the manufacturer in 1998. One aircraft was assigned to Aero Caribbean as CU-T1298, but later re-registered as CU-T1512. CU-T1298 had previously been allocated to an Aero Caribbean Yak-40. The Yak-40 was withdrawn from service in 2018 and is now preserved at the fire station in the Havana district of Capdevila. Three ATR-72s were later acquired. In 2006, an ATR-72, CU-T1548, was the first to be received and was initially operated by Aero Caribbean. In July 2015, it was transferred to Cubana and later received a 'C' check and returned to service. The third aircraft, CU-T1549, went directly to Aero Caribbean and was in the company's colours when it crashed on 4 November 2010, while on a scheduled flight from Santiago de Cuba to Havana.

Additionally, during that year, a number of A319 and A320s were leased from Avion Express, a leasing company based in Lithuania, to operate the short and medium-haul flights between early 1998 and February 2002.

In 2004, Cubana began a long-term renovation programme, including the renovation of the IL-62M fleet to use on its international routes. Cubana had a programme to spend US$100m per year on Soviet-built aircraft over a period of eight years. This strategy was also designed to include an upgrade of its technical support ability. As part of this, the airline formed a joint venture company, in a 50/50 shareholding, with the Spanish airline Iberia in 2005. This enabled them to maintain and perform heavier maintenance checks on Airbus and Boeing aircraft for third party carriers. In the same year, a Yak-42D, RA-42444, was leased from Tatarstan Air, re-registered as CU-T1249, and stayed in service with the airline until 2007.

Cubana inherited three EMB-110 Bandeirantes from Aero Caribbean following the takeover in 2015. After this one made a belly landing at Havana, they were withdrawn from service. (Cuban Civil Aviation Authority)

Cubana operated four IL-96-300s. This one is on approach to Havana in May 2016. (Gerry Manning)

In July 2004, Cubana placed an order for two IL-96-300s, (CU-T1250 and -1251), reportedly at a cost of US$110m. Of the costs, 85 per cent was financed by Roseximbank, a Russian state-owned organisation, which provides financial and guarantee support to its exporters. Cuba's Aviaimport, a state-owned civil aviation company that specialises in foreign trade, particularly with Russia, provided the remaining 15 per cent. The order represented the first sale of the aircraft outside the former Soviet Union. The first aircraft was delivered in December 2005.

In April 2006, another deal was signed for the purchase of a further two IL96-300s and two Tupolev Tu-204s. This deal was worth US$250m. Of the Tu-204s, one was specifically for cargo, and designated Tu-204-100CE. These were received by Cubana in June and August of 2007. Also in August 2007, Cubana signed a memorandum of understanding for two further Tu-204s and three Antonov An-158s. However, one of the Tu-204 freighter orders was cancelled, because the financier, Russia's Vneshtorgbank, wanted to charge a higher interest rate than the 7–8 per cent that had been approved by both governments.

Cubana had now settled on the An-158 as the replacement for the Yaks on its domestic and short-haul routes, and it placed an order for three of the type in 2012. As the third aircraft was

Originally delivered in December 2005, CU-T1250 is possibly one of the last operating IL-96s of those delivered. (Gerry Manning)

delivered in 2013, a further order for three aircraft was placed, to be delivered in 2014. A further order was placed in 2013 by the airline, this time for three IL-96-400s. This, in a typical two-class configuration, would have capacity for about 386 passengers. In the event, only 16 of the type were built, of which just ten ever flew. Production was not continued, and thus Cubana never took delivery of these aircraft.

Despite the relationship between Cuba and the former Soviet Union nations continuing long into the 21st century, on 3 June 2009, the Organisation of American States adopted a resolution that gave Cuba the opportunity to end the 47-year ban on its membership. However, Fidel Castro stated that he was not interested in rejoining the group.

Aero Caribbean had been established in 1982 as a wholly government-owned airline, primarily to operate some domestic flights and regional charters as a supplemental airline to Cubana. It had always co-operated closely with Cubana, and in 2015 it was merged with the national carrier. The merger brought about a significant change in Cubana's fleet, adding three ATR-42-300s, and four ATR 72-200s, together with four Embraer 110 Bandeirantes. There was also an IL-18 in the Aero Caribbean fleet, but it was never actually transferred to Cubana.

In 2017, Cubana leased two of the four ATR 72s, from South African lessor Solenta Aviation, principally to operate the domestic and short-haul routes, but the aircraft proved to be a poor replacement for the An-158 fleet. The aircraft had a smaller seating capacity and were only able to achieve a 50 per cent reliability rate, with, in some cases, passengers waiting up to 12 hours for a flight, only for it to be eventually cancelled and having to travel by bus. The May 2018 accident further disrupted Cubana's schedules that had already been subject to significant disruption, with flights failing to operate for various reasons given by the airline. Just two months after the accident, almost 180 Canadian tourists were stranded for three days in Cayo Coco. The reason given on the day of departure was inclement weather, but no explanation was given for the remainder of the delay. It was known that domestic flights were being cancelled, and passengers frequently had to make their journey by bus. The aircraft scheduled for the domestic flights were being used to operate flights to Guyana and Haiti.

Another blow to the domestic operation came about in 2018, when the An-158s had to be grounded because of a lack of spare parts – a common problem with aircraft built in the former Soviet Union, as we have discussed. But the problem with spare parts was not the only difficulty the airline was facing with this aircraft. Many of the onboard systems, most of them computer driven, were not working correctly, and following this, the Cuban authorities withdrew the Antonov's Certificate of Airworthiness.

Much of the carrier's wide-body and narrow-body Soviet-era jet fleet awaits 'C'-checks, which Moscow had agreed to finance. However, disagreements between the Russian lessor IFC, the manufacturers and key vendors in Ukraine, together with Russian activities in Ukraine, have soured relations between Moscow and Kyiv and thus delayed the process.

At the Moscow Air Show in 2007, CU-T1701 was proudly displayed as the first export sale of the Tu-204. However, this -100 Series aircraft was withdrawn from service just nine years later. (Gerry Manning)

The third of four Tu-204s, Cubana later took delivery of the Series 200CE version. CU-C1703 lands at Panama's Tocumen Airport. (Gerry Manning)

Officials at Cubana frequently blame the embargo for delays and cancellations, and it is known that there have been numerous problems with the operation of the An-158. However, these are clearly not the only causes. The weekly flight to Paris was suspended in January 2018, despite that fact that it was using a chartered aircraft from French carrier Air Caraïbes, which had begun its flights to the Island at the end of 2016, in a codeshare with Cubana. The regular flight to Santo Domingo had been cancelled a few weeks previously. At the time, all but one of the IL-96s were unserviceable, with the remaining aircraft operating the route to Caracas and Buenos Aires. The twice-weekly route between Havana and Madrid was being operated by a chartered Airbus A340 operated by Plus Ultra Lineas Aéreas, a Spanish charter company.

The crash, with the loss of all on board, on 18 May 2018 of a leased Boeing 737-200 belonging to Mexican carrier Aerolíneas Damojh on a domestic flight between Havana and Holguin, simply served to exacerbate Cubana's problems, and the government ordered the airline to suspend all operations with foreign-leased aircraft until further notice. The accident became a huge scandal, primarily within Cuba, since most of the passengers were Cuban, but also in the wider Latin American and Caribbean region, leaving a very poor international impression of Cubana's standards. This left Cubana with hardly any aircraft with which to operate services, with the former Soviet aircraft all withdrawn from service and no prospect of replacements, and Cubana was left with no alternative but to suspend both its domestic and international flights.

On 27 December 2018, the Russian aircraft manufacturer Voronezh Aircraft Company revealed the amount paid by Cubana for 14 Russian and Ukrainian aircraft since 2006: US$432m. Despite the fact that these were new aircraft, many were soon grounded owing to technical problems. At that time, of the carrier's four IL-96-300s, just one, CU-T1250, was operational, having been in Voronezh for more than a year for a major check. A second aircraft, CU-T1251 needed a replacement nosewheel undercarriage unit before it could be returned to service. The third aircraft, CU-T1254, has been in storage in Havana for some time. Voronezh has said that the aircraft is unserviceable and would need to be ferried back to the manufacturer for a major engineering check. The fourth aircraft, CU-T1717, is also in storage and seems unlikely to fly in the foreseeable future. The An-158s are discussed elsewhere in the chapter.

Three of the largest aircraft manufacturers, Airbus, ATR and Boeing, were approached to see if they could offer aircraft, but the fact that they contained more than 10 per cent of US components meant that Cubana would be unable to successfully operate them. In September 2018, Cubana declared that the US embargo, coupled with the limitations on banking transactions and the movement of foreign currency, meant that they had no option but to lease aircraft from third parties. For example, a Boeing 737-300, I-BPAG, was leased from Blue Panorama between December 2018 and October 2019 to operate flights to Venezuela and Peru. For the Madrid route, Cubana briefly leased a Boeing 767-300, S9-DBY, from EuroAtlantic Airways. By January of 2019, new flights had begun to the French Caribbean islands of Guadeloupe and Martinique, and some domestic flights were also resumed.

Among various types of Russian aircraft, Cubana continues to operate some Western aircraft, including the turboprop ATR-42s and -72s from Avions de Transport Régional, and three EMB-110

CU-T1702, a Tu-204-100E passenger version, arrives at Havana in May 2016. (Gerry Manning)

Another view of CU-T1701 as it awaits its next flight in Panama. (Gerry Manning)

Bandeirantes from Embraer. Of these, CU-T1541 suffered damage following a belly landing in Havana on 28 November 2020, following a flight from Isla de la Juventud. Soon after this, all three aircraft, which had been used for domestic flights, were taken out of service. The first two Bandeirantes had first been operated by Aerotaxi, a small state-owned company, in late 2001 and registered as CU-T1108 and CU-T1109. CU-T1108 was re-registered as CU-T1540 in 2003 and then transferred to Aero Caribbean in 2009. CU-T1109 became CU-T1541 when it was transferred to Aero Caribbean in 2009. The third aircraft was received by Aero Caribbean in August 2007 and registered CU-T1551. Following the merger in 2015, all the aircraft became part of the Cubana fleet.

Under the Obama administration between 2009 and 2017, the US and Cuba both reopened embassies, thus providing full diplomatic representation and the relaxing of many restrictions that had been in place since the embargo began, and there were expectations that finally the sanctions would start to be eased. However, when the Trump administration took over in 2017, it enacted 243 measures against Cuba, the most in decades, including 50 which were imposed during the COVID-19 pandemic. He also reinforced travel restrictions, and in a final rebuke named Cuba a state sponsor of terrorism. The Biden administration, in power at the time of writing, appears to have little or no interest in reviving the relationship. Cuban President Miguel Díaz-Canel has called on President Biden to repeal Trump's moves. President Biden answered a question from reporters about reinstating internet access to Cuba, saying 'We're considering whether we have the technological ability to reinstate that access'.

In August 2021, the IATA, of which Cubana was a founding member, suspended the airline from the Billing Settlement Plan (BSP) revenue system, in the belief that the carrier was at risk of bankruptcy or the cessation of operations. The BSP is an IATA accounting system that simplifies the transfer of monies between IATA accredited passenger sales agents, travel agents and airlines, thus allowing the transfer of different currencies quickly and securely between the parties concerned. The suspension makes it very difficult for Cubana to sell electronic tickets. A director of the airline, Arsenio Arocha, explained the financial difficulties that the company was going through, adding that one major problem the airline had was its inability to lease aircraft or access international credits in order to maintain its aircraft. In addition, it had been forced to close bank accounts in Santo Domingo, Panama, Paris and Madrid, all of them major destinations on Cubana's network. Atocha suggested that the US policy towards Cuba limited the financial flow of the company and contributed to the losses suffered during the COVID-19 pandemic.

The COVID-19 pandemic hit Cubana in the same way as every other airline. Despite tourism being the country's primary source of foreign income, the government closed the island's borders. The effect was devastating. In 2020, during the height of the crisis, the IL-96s were used to collect shipments from Shanghai and transport them, via Moscow and Gander, to Havana, but the few routes that were still being operated generated very little money for the airline. The country is believed to have

Tu-204 CU-T1701 arrives in Havana. This aircraft was returned to Ulyanovsk and has recently emerged in a new colour scheme. (EcuRed)

The Coopesa hangars of San Jose, Costa Rica, form the background as CU-T1711 takes off. (Gerry Manning)

lost US$5.5bn, and Cubana itself, during the two years during which the pandemic was prevalent, is believed to have lost US$353m.

A more recent problem for Cubana has been the war in Ukraine. During the early days of the Russian invasion of Ukraine, the Antonov factory in Gostomel, near Kyiv, was the scene of a fierce battle between Russian and Ukrainian troops. During this, the factory, and the aircraft within it, sustained serious damage, and thus the provision of spares and maintenance is at a standstill.

So where does this leave the US traveller who wants to fly to Cuba for their holidays? The short answer is that it is difficult. Even in mid-2022, tourism, as such, to the island is prohibited. There are certain exceptions: prospective travellers have to book accommodation in Cuba only in guest houses and not major hotels, and they cannot stay at any accommodation listed in the very long Cuba Prohibited Accommodations List or spend money with any non-approved businesses within Cuba. All records and receipts for the journey must be kept for five years. This is inconvenient for Cuban-Americans who wish to visit friends and relations in Cuba, but for American tourists simply wanting to visit Cuba for tourism purposes alone, this is a considerable disincentive, when they can travel to so many other islands in the Caribbean with no restrictions whatsoever.

Any visitor to Havana's Jose Marti Airport in mid-2020 would find little activity with the Cubana fleet. The routes that it formerly operated have now been taken over by an assortment of other carriers. The route to Santo Domingo (Dominican Republic) is operated by Air Century, which is based there.

CU-T1711, one of six An-158s delivered to Cubana, takes off from San Jose, Costa Rica. All six aircraft are currently out of service awaiting parts that have been delayed by the war in Ukraine. (Gerry Manning)

This Air Outre Mer DC-10-30, F-GNEM, was leased to operate Cubana's long-haul routes between November 1992 and July 1993. (EcuRed)

In more recent times, Cubana has leased a number of types from different operators. A320-321 EI-TLJ operated for the company between November 1998 and October 2000. (Malcolm Nason)

Built in 1995, this ATR-72 is one of the few aircraft still flying with Cubana. It is seen here landing in Antigua. (Björn Düwel)

The Cancun flight is operated by low-cost carrier Viva Aerobus, with Copa flying to Panama City and Conviasa to Caracas. Routes to the US are operated by American Airlines, iAero (formerly Swift Air), Jet Blue and Southwest Airlines. At the time of writing, there are almost 100 flights a week between Havana and various points in Florida, though not operated by Cubana.

American Airlines has recently been given permission to operate to additional destinations in Cuba, such as Camagüey, Cayo Coco, Cayo Largo, Cienfuegos, Holguín, Manzanillo, Matanzas, Santa Clara and Santiago. These routes had previously been authorised by the Obama administration, then rescinded under President Trump. The principal beneficiaries of these flights will be Cuban-Americans, who have previously had to use charter flights, or fly to Havana and then use surface transport to reach their destinations. Despite the additional routes authorised to US carriers, Cubana is, of course, prevented from operating reciprocal services because of the ongoing embargo. The long-established route to Buenos Aires is operated weekly with the lone operational IL-96. Services to Madrid are operated by World2Fly with an A350-900, Iberia with an A330-200 and Air Europa with a B787-800. Cubana is still operating some domestic services, using ATR 72s leased from Solenta Aviation in South Africa. The An-128s are grounded, with what have been described as 'technical difficulties' and a shortage of spares.

So, what of the future for Cubana? Will it be able to celebrate its centenary in 2029? Currently, there are only a few airworthy aircraft in the fleet. The grounded An-158s are unlikely to be made airworthy again in the short term. The 'technical difficulties' with the fleet of six aircraft, most of which are only eight years old, cannot be dealt with as long as the current war in Ukraine continues. These aircraft were intended to operate the domestic and short-haul flights, and as a result, the domestic flights are

By no means the first aircraft to carry this temporary registration, this aircraft was initially delivered to Aerogaviota in VIP configuration in 2002 and became CU-T1240. Note the red propeller covers. (EcuRed)

only operating sporadically, and, as described above, the short-haul routes have been taken over by other operators based outside Cuba. Since diplomatic relations between Russia and Cuba are cordial, there is talk of holiday flights resuming during the coming European winter. Given that there are currently travel restrictions in place to many European destinations for Russians, and Cuba has always been a popular location for them, this would be an ideal opportunity to reintroduce the route. There is no indication that the US will lift any of the embargo restrictions in the foreseeable future, and even if they did, it is unlikely that Cubana would have the aircraft or the finance to enable them to lease aircraft to operate the routes. The long-haul flights are being carried out by aircraft from a number of different charter operators, but, despite having received a subsidy of more than €200,000 from the Community of Madrid, there seems to be little likelihood of Cubana's aircraft taking part in the schedules being operated by foreign carriers.

From a general travel perspective, the worst effects of the COVID-19 pandemic have now passed, and it is to be hoped that Cubana can undergo some form of restructuring, which will allow the carrier to operate a more comprehensive and reliable schedule on both its domestic and international routes, thus enabling it to acquire some much-needed revenue and head more securely towards its centenary.

An example of the DC-8-43 that crashed off the coast of Barbados after bombs had been placed on board. (Pierre Langlois via urrib2000)

Hijacking and Accidents

Hijacking and terrorism

Hijacking became synonymous with various forms of air terrorism beginning in the late 1950s. A few of the major incidents are recalled in the following paragraphs.

On 1 November 1958, a Viscount 755D, CU-T603, was operating flight 495 between Miami and Varadero. The aircraft did not arrive at its destination and was later found badly damaged in the Bahía de Nipe, very close to the airport at Preston. It was reported in the press that the flight had been hijacked by five men, identified as members of the 'July 26 Movement' (M-26-7), who had put on their uniforms mid-flight and announced that the aircraft was going to be diverted to the eastern region of Cuba. The intention was for it to land at Preston Airport, a town some 375 miles (600km) southeast of Veradero, which at the time lay in an area controlled by anti-Batista rebels. At this time, during the revolution, Veradero was still under the control of President Batista. It is believed that the aircraft was trying to land at Preston Airport when it ran out of fuel on final approach. The aircraft was carrying weapons and ammunition allegedly destined for the rebels who were hiding in the Sierra Maestra mountains, where Fidel Castro, accompanied by his brother Raúl and other members of the M-26-7 rebel movement, including Che Guevara, were preparing to deal the final blow against the government of Fulgencio Batista. The airport is no longer open. It is worth noting that Preston, named after one of the founders of the US-based United Fruit Company, was renamed as Guatemala following the revolution, in order to show solidarity with the Central American nation.

On 29 October 1960, flight 905, operated by a DC-3, departed Havana on a domestic flight to Nueva Gerona on Isla de la Juventud (Isle of Youth). About ten minutes after take-off, the co-pilot reportedly jumped up, grabbed the air marshal, and forced the pilot at gunpoint to head to Key West in the US. A shooting took place, and the air marshal was killed. A total of nine people participated in the hijack and requested political asylum in the US. Two additional passengers joined them in their request.

On 8 December 1960, a Cubana aircraft, type unknown, crashed near Cienfuegos during a domestic flight to Havana, following an attempt by five Cubans to hijack the aircraft to the US. A gun battle erupted, and one person was killed, prior to the crash-landing of the aircraft.

On 3 July 1961, a DC-3, registration unknown, was operating a domestic flight between Havana and Varadero, when 14 passengers hijacked the aircraft and demanded to be flown to Miami, where it landed later. The aircraft was subsequently returned.

On 9 August 1961, a C-46, registration unknown, was operating a flight between Havana and Nueva Gerona, when five Cubans attempted a hijacking. There were two security guards on the aircraft, who attempted to stop the hijack, but the ensuing gun battle killed the captain, a guard and one of the hijackers. The aircraft made an emergency landing in a sugar cane field, and the remaining hijackers fled the scene.

On 27 March 1966, an IL-18, registration CU-T831, was performing a domestic flight from Santiago de Cuba to Havana with 97 persons on board. After take-off, the flight engineer shot dead the security guard and tried to force the pilots to fly the aircraft to the US. Instead, the pilot continued to Havana. Upon landing, the hijacker saw an Aeroflot aircraft and, realising he had been tricked, shot dead the pilot and tried to initiate a take-off, but the co-pilot shut down the engines. He was attacked and seriously injured, following which the hijacker jumped onto the tarmac and fled. The hijacker was later caught and executed.

In July 1976, flight CU-455, a scheduled flight operating from Georgetown (Guyana) to Havana, via Trinidad, Barbados and Kingston (Jamaica), had been targeted using a bomb in a suitcase, but this exploded shortly before it was loaded onto the aircraft in Kingston. However, the terrorists were determined, and, on 6 October 1976, attempted to attack the same flight. The aircraft, CU-T1201, a DC-8-43 that Cubana had leased from Air Canada, was operating flight CU-455. The aircraft took off from what was then known as Seawell Airport in Barbados, heading for its next destination of Kingston. Having climbed to an altitude of 18,000ft (5,846m), a bomb, situated in a rear lavatory, exploded. The pilots immediately called Seawell, explaining that there had been an explosion on board, and that they were returning to the airport. As they did this, a second bomb exploded in the mid-section of the passenger cabin. The lavatory explosion destroyed the aircraft's control cables, and the second one blew a large hole in the aircraft, following which there was a fire. The pilots, realising that a successful landing would now be impossible, turned the aircraft back out to sea, rather than endanger the lives of the tourists relaxing on a nearby beach. The aircraft went into a rapid descent and crashed into the sea about 5 miles (8km) short of the airport. All 73 innocent people on board were killed, including all the members of the Cuban national fencing team, and a monument commemorating the event was erected at Porters, in the district of St James, near to where the aircraft crashed.

On 11 March 1987, an An-24RV, CU-T1262, was operating flight CU-706 between Havana and Nueva Gerona, when three passengers attempted to hijack the flight. There were 48 people on board. The hijackers used hand grenades and demanded to be flown to the US. In the ensuing melee with other passengers, a grenade exploded, injuring 13 people. One hijacker was killed by a police officer who was on board the aircraft, and the other two were arrested.

On 4 January 1992, in one of the less 'dramatic' hijackings, a Cuban pilot commandeered a helicopter from Varadero Airport about 50 miles (80km) from Havana and flew it to an area about 15 miles (24km) away, where he picked up 33 relatives and friends and flew them to Tamiami Airport in Florida. The aircraft was a Mil Mi-8, registration CU-H407, and part of Cubana's fleet, and it had originally been scheduled to take tourists on a flight around the island. The pilot apparently fooled guards and air traffic controllers at Varadero Airport by dressing his brother-in-law and another man in spare uniforms and boarding the Cubana helicopter for what he told the airport staff was to be a routine flight. He then flew the aircraft at low level towards the US, with the flight taking about 80 minutes, but it was picked up by radar as it approached the Florida Keys, and a Blackhawk helicopter and a fixed-wing aircraft then escorted them to Tamiami airfield. The passengers asked for, and were given, political asylum in the US. The aircraft was put on display at the airport before being later returned to Cuba.

On 7 June 1996, a Cubana An-2, with ten passengers on board, was hijacked as it was flying from Bayamo in southern Cuba to Santiago de Cuba. Lieutenant Colonel José Pupo demanded at gunpoint for the aircraft to land at the US Naval Base at Guantanamo. He was tried in a US court on 29 May 1997 and found not guilty.

Accidents

The lack of accurate navigational aids in both the air and on the ground and inadequate weather forecasting were significant factors in accidents everywhere during the early years of aviation. People tend to think of the weather in the Caribbean as being benign, but it can be subject to sudden changes and violent meteorological conditions, to say nothing of hurricanes in the third quarter of the year.

One of the worst and earliest accidents was with a DC-4, CU-T397, which, while on a flight from Madrid to Havana on 6 December 1952, made a stop at Kindley Field, Bermuda. It had arrived at Bermuda from Santa Maria, Azores, at 0330hrs for a refuelling stop. The aircraft crashed into the sea shortly after take-off from Kindley Field. No conclusive cause for the accident was ever established.

On 25 April 1951, CU-T188, a DC-4, was on a flight from Miami to Havana and was taking up a heading for Havana, when it was in collision with a US Navy SNB-1 Kansan, which was on an instrument training flight from Key West Naval Station, Florida. The Kansan crashed into the sea just north of the Naval Air Station, but the DC-4 was able to continue for some distance before it went into a steep nose-down left bank and crashed into the sea 1.7 miles (2.7km) from the site of the collision.

On 18 May 2018, a Boeing 737-200, XA-UHZ, crashed while taking off from Havana, having begun its operations in Cuba on 14 May 2018. The aircraft did not belong to Cubana, it had been wet-leased (i.e., the aircraft, crew, maintenance and insurance are all included in the lease costs) from a Mexican airline, Global Air, to fill a gap in the current operating capabilities of Cubana. The aircraft was almost 39 years old at the time of the accident, with almost 70,000 hours in the logbook. On the day of the accident, the aircraft flew from Havana to Santiago de Cuba and back, arriving at Havana at 1020hrs local time. The next flight on the programme was flight CU 972 to Holguín, with a scheduled departure time of 1100hrs. During the preparation for this flight, the usual calculations were made for take-off weight and weight distribution. However, the cabin configuration on the loadsheet differed from the actual configuration of XA-UHZ. Based on these data, the centre of gravity was incorrectly calculated, meaning that the aircraft was out of trim, thus resulting in the incorrect balance of the aircraft prior to take-off. The aircraft taxied to the runway for departure, and after receiving clearance for take-off, began to accelerate down runway 06. As soon as it rotated from the runway, the aircraft attained a nose-high and right-wing low attitude. The ground proximity warning system began to sound in the cockpit: 'Bank angle, bank angle!' The bank angle reached 35 degrees before the aircraft rolled back. It banked right and left several times with the nose reaching about 30 degrees nose up. The crew issued a Mayday call. The aircraft lost speed and began an uncontrolled descent until it impacted the ground about 40 seconds after lifting off the runway. The aircraft came down in vegetation near a railway line outside the airport, broke up and burst into flames. There were 107 passengers on board, together with six Mexican crew members. Three passengers initially survived the accident. One survivor died on 21 May and a second died on 25 May. Cubana had previously leased XA-UBB, a similar aircraft, from the same company between March and September 2009.

Cubana's Soviet-built Aircraft

Cuba is unique in having operated the only significant Soviet-built passenger fleet outside the Soviet Union, and it is appropriate to record the details, where they are known, of the aircraft that served with Cubana. The following table records the known details of those aircraft, both fixed-wing and helicopters, in order of registration.

Some further words of explanation are required regarding the construction numbers used in the following tables. Under the systems employed by the Soviet Union, manufacturing of one type of aircraft often took place at various different sites, which were usually denoted by a three-letter prefix, followed by further numbers indicating the batch, the year and finally the sequence number on the production line. These can sometimes run into ten or 12 digits, so here the system has been simplified in most cases to show only the last numbers, using the same construction number system as that used by Western manufacturers.

Cuba uses an unusual registration system, which also requires some explanation. The early aircraft, including the Ford Trimotors and Lockheed L10 Electras, used an 'NM' prefix, followed by a number sequence. For example, the original Curtiss Robin operated was NM-1. This system was changed to the 'CU-' prefix in 1945:

- 'CU-A' Agricultural aircraft
- 'CU-C' Cargo aircraft
- 'CU-D' Sport aircraft (not currently used)
- 'CU-H' Helicopters
- 'CU-P' Private aircraft
- 'CU-T' Passenger carrying aircraft
- 'CU-U' Ultralights and historic aircraft
- 'CU-X' Experimental

Here is a list of abbreviations used below:

A/F	Air Force
b/u	Broken up
cfit	Controlled flight into terrain (note that terrain also includes water)
c/n	Constructor's number
c/s	Colours
d/d	Delivered
dbr	Damaged beyond repair
f/f	First flight
mfd	Manufactured
n/k	Not known

ntu   Not taken up

rts   Returned to service

wfu   Withdrawn from use

w/o   Written off

CU-T321: lL-14P. VIP version. No further details.

CU-T322: IL-14T c/n 1642. Military transport version. Also reported as CU-T822, the aircraft was w/o 13 May 1980 on a training flight from Varadero. As the crew practised stalls, the aircraft entered a left spin and they were unable to recover it, so that the aircraft crashed into the sea some 540 yards (0.5km) off Varadero Beach.

CU-H402: Mi-8 c/n 40725. Originally delivered to Cubana and based in Varadero, later transferred to Aerogaviota.

CU-H404: Mi-8T c/n 40726. D/d Dec 1991. Originally delivered to Cubana but transferred to Aerogaviota in Nov 1997.

CU-H403: Mi-8T c/n 40727. D/d 1991. Originally delivered to Cubana but transferred to Aerogaviota in 1998.

CU-H407: Mi 8T c/n 33011. D/d to Cubana in Nov 1991. On 2 Jan 1992, the helicopter was flown to an area outside the airfield, where it collected 30 passengers and flew to Tamiami Airport in Florida. Further details in Appendix 1. It was subsequently transferred to Aerogaviota.

A general view of the AN-2 base at Santa Fé. (Jan Kopp)

CU-H410: Mi-8T c/n 40733. D/d to Cubana prior to 1980 and went to Aerogaviota in 1991.

CU-H414: Mi-8 c/n 40728. Still on the register in 1995.

CU-H417: Mi-8P c/n 40740. D/d 1987. Still on the register in 1995.

CU-H418: Mi-8P c/n 40741. D/d 1988. Still on the register in 1995.

CU-H419: Mi-8P c/n 40742. D/d 1989. Still on the register in 1995.

CU-H420: Mi-8P c/n 40743. D/d to Cubana in 1990. The last of the first-generation Mi-8 delivered to Cuba. Still on the register in 1995.

CU-T814: IL-14 c/n n/k. No other details.

CU-T815: IL-14 c/n n/k. No other details.

CU-T816: IL-14M c/n 1239. D/d Oct 1961. Originally CCCP-L1561, later CCCP-91561 and to Cuba as CU-T816. Preserved at Santiago de Cuba. Last seen in Mar 2001 and Feb 2002 with 'Club Juvenil' titles. B/u Feb 2012.

CU-T817: IL-14 c/n n/k. No other details.

CU-T818: IL-14M c/n n/k. No other details.

CU-T819: IL-14 c/n n/k. W/o 27 Mar 1962 during a flight from Santiago de Cuba to Havana, when it crashed into the Cayman Trough some 1.5km off the coast shortly after take-off.

CU-T820: IL-14 c/n n/k. Seen Oct 1981. Originally preserved in the Lenin Park in Havana.

CU-T821: IL-14M c/n n/k. No other details.

CU-T822: IL-14 c/n n/k. See CU-T322.

CU-T823: IL-14 c/n n/k. No other details.

CU-T824: IL-14P c/n n/k. VIP version (salon); reported to be the personal aircraft used by Raul Castro. It was shot down near the town of Jaruco, 40 miles (65km) from Havana, on 19 Jun 1965, in error by a Cuban SA-2 missile.

CU-T825: IL-14P c/n n/k. VIP version (salon); reported to be the personal aircraft used by Fidel Castro. Seen 21 Nov 1997 preserved in the DAFAAR (armed forces) museum.

CU-T827: An-12A c/n 1504. D/d 1962. The aircraft was built to the same specifications as a batch of Indian A/F aircraft that were in production at the same time, and was fitted with the glass rear turret, but demilitarised. While performing a non-scheduled cargo flight from Havana to Mexico

CU-A1800 sits outside the hangar. (Jan Kopp)

City on 9 Feb 1967, the aircraft crashed while on approach to the airport at Mexico City. It was carrying out a non-scheduled international cargo flight. The crew had contacted the Mexico Control Centre and requested authorisation to enter Mexican airspace. This was granted, and the latest weather information for Mexico City Airport was transmitted to the aircraft, but no acknowledgement was received. Subsequent transmissions from the aircraft were unintelligible, and the crew were instructed to change to another frequency. The clearance and weather information were again passed to the aircraft on that frequency. The crew confirmed their positions over various reporting points and were informed that visibility at Mexico City was 1.5 miles (2.4km) in fog. They were then instructed to descend from 18,000ft to 12,000ft (5,486m to 3,658m), and to contact the approach controller. The crew were also advised that the runway would be 23L and that the wind was calm. At 0458hrs, the crew reported over the VOR leaving 11,000ft (3,353m) and were instructed to contact the tower controller. This was the last contact with the aircraft. It did not establish contact on the tower frequency. The aircraft struck some ploughed land about 11 miles (18km) from the end of runway 23L. The aircraft completely disintegrated. The subsequent investigation revealed that the crew had executed an IFR descent procedure other than that which was established for Mexico City International Airport. Cfit. W/o.

CU-T830: IL-18V c/n 4905. Originally CCCP-75826. Left the Soviet Union in Sep 1962 on lease and arrived at Havana in early Jul 1963 after stopovers at Belgrade, Algiers, Conakry, Recife and Port of Spain; dbr 10 Jul 1966 on a flight from Havana to Santiago de Cuba when it suffered a multiple engine failure and made a forced landing near Cienfuegos, suffering severe damage. W/o.

CU-T831: IL-18V c/n 5202. Originally CCCP-75836 and d/d in 1964, it was named *Capitán Fernando Alvarez*, in honour of the captain who was killed during the hijack attempt on board this aircraft on 27 Mar 1966. Wfu Havana 1984.

CU-T832: IL-18Gr (cargo version) c/n 5501. D/d 1964. Originally CCCP-75843; converted to an IL-18V in Oct 1968. Later delivered to Fits Air and became UR-CFR.

CU-T875: An-24 c/n 2402. D/d May 1966. Flown to Leningrad from the Antonov factory near Kyiv in May 1966, it was disassembled before being transported by sea to Cuba, where it was re-assembled at Ciudad Libertad. Presumably, the early versions did not have the range to fly the northern route – Iceland, Greenland, Canada, etc. W/o 29 Aug 1966 at Camagüey while doing crew training. Both engines failed due to fuel starvation owing to the crew's unfamiliarity with the fuel system. The aircraft crashed just under 5,000ft (1500m) short of the runway.

CU-T876: An-24V c/n 2403. D/d by sea in Mar 1966. During scheduled flight CU 707 from Nueva Gerona to Havana on 14 May 1973, the aircraft crashed whilst landing at Havana. There was bad weather at the time. Dbr.

CU-T877: An-24V c/n 2404. D/d by sea in 1966. It was seen in poor condition in Jul 1999. Wfu and b/u.

CU-T878: An-24V c/n 2410. D/d by sea in 1966. Last flight reported as 24 Dec 93. Wfu Havana and scrapped shortly afterwards.

CU-T879: An-24V c/n 2501. D/d by sea in Mar 1966 and w/o 18 Mar 1976, following a mid-air collision near Havana during a crew training exercise prior to an air show, with Cubana DC-8 CU-T1200. The outer portion of the DC-8's wing and No.1 engine separated from the aircraft, but the DC-8 was able to land safely.

CU-T880: An-24V c/n 2502. D/d by sea in 1966. This was the initial export version of the An-24B 50-seat airliner, with the early narrow chord inner wings, double-slotted flaps, single ventral fin and power provided by two 2,550hp (1,902kW) Ivchenko AI-24A turboprop engines. Wfu 1974. Seen preserved in Lenin Park between Dec 1995 and Feb 2014, but front fuselage only, with rear fuselage burnt. Since b/u.

CU-T881: An-24V c/n 2601. D/d by sea in 1966. Salon version with improved wide chord inner wings. In service 1966–Jul 1997. Wfu.

CU-T882: An-24V c/n 2603. D/d by sea in 1966; re-assembled by Oct 1966. Built as a saloon version and widely used by DDR leader Erich Honecker during a state visit to Cuba. Transferred to Aero Caribbean in early 1995 and later re-registered CU-T1500.

CU-F888: IL-14T c/n u/k. Little info, but a black and white photo exists, showing a small lightning-bolt cheatline. Possibly only used for cargo.

CU-T899: lL-18D c/n 1102. D/d Dec 1968. W/o 19 Jan 1985 near San Jose de los Lajas, 17m (30km) from Havana, following an engine fire on take-off on a flight between Havana and Managua, Nicaragua.

CU-C900: IL-18D c/n 1104. D/d in Dec 1968. Transferred to Aero Caribbean in Dec 1991. Converted to IL-18Gr (cargo configuration) in Apr 1991 (*Gruzovoy* is the Russian word for cargo) and transferred to Aero Caribbean in Dec 1991. In operation until Nov 1999. Wfu in order to become a restaurant.

CU-T925: IL-14FKM c/n 3202. D/d Jun 1973 and converted to IL-14 FKM (aerial photography version). Originally CCCP-L1523 as an IL-14M, then CCCP-91523. Seen Havana in Sep 1984 with Groza-40 weather radar (nose cone housing from a Yak-40). Re-registered as CU-T925 for Aero Caribbean in 1984. Wfu in 1999 and then installed in Santiago de Cuba as a youth club, later b/u.

CU-T1202: Yak-40S2 c/n 1449. D/d by sea to Santiago de Cuba and re-assembled in early Nov 1976. During a scheduled flight from Camagüey to Santiago de Cuba at night, on 24 Oct 1990, the aircraft had to go around twice due to poor weather (rain and reduced visibility). An NDB approach was flown to runway 09, but the approach was abandoned at 0151hrs. A second attempt was made at 0155hrs, resulting in another aborted approach. The crew then attempted to manoeuvre visually for an approach to runway 27. The aircraft crashed into mountainous terrain at Punta Jardinero, 2.5 miles (4km) short of the threshold of runway 27. Cfit. W/o.

CU-T1203: Yak-40 c/n 1450. D/d by sea to Santiago de Cuba and re-assembled during early Nov 1976. Seen in Prague in 1991 in all-white c/s. Registered as YV-598C in Nov 1995; reg then cancelled and Cuban reg restored prior to delivery to Aero Caribbean in 1998.

CU-T1204: (1) Yak-40 c/n 1650. D/d by sea to Santiago de Cuba and re-assembled during early Nov 1976. Wfu. Not in the fleet list in Dec 2005. B/u. Identity assumed by c/n 1260 for preservation purposes.

CU-T1206: Yak-40 c/n 1049 (not confirmed – possibly 1249). D/d by sea to Santiago de Cuba and assembled Nov 1976. To Cuban A/F as 12-41. Then believed registered as CU-T1441, but still with A/F. Seen in Apr 1996 in DAAFAR museum as FAR 14-41 with Fuerza Aérea Revolucionaria titles. Later moved to San Antonio de los Baños Air Base, south of Havana, but believed to be dismantled.

CU-T1207: Yak-40 c/n 1445. D/d by sea to Santiago de Cuba and re-assembled during May 1977. Initially to Cuban A/F as 12-42, but later registered to Cubana as CU-T1440. Stored in Playa Baracoa in 2003, and b/u there some years later.

CU-T1208: IL-62M c/n 6739. D/d Jun 1977. It was named *Captain Wilfredo Perez* in honour of a Cubana pilot who was killed when his aircraft was sabotaged. Last flight was Jan 1992; noted in Havana Nov 1996 wfu; not in the 1998 fleet list. B/u.

CU-T1209: IL-62M c/n 8132. D/d Jan 1978. Last flight 30 Jun 1996. Seen in Havana Jul 1999 wfu; not in 2001 fleet list. B/u.

CU-T1211: Yak-40 c/n 1554. D/d by sea to Santiago de Cuba and re-assembled by May 1977. Transferred to Aero Caribbean in 1995.

CU-T1212: Yak-40 c/n 1954. D/d by sea to Santiago de Cuba and re-assembled by May 1977. Transferred to Aero Caribbean in 1991.

CU-T1213: Yak-40 c/n 1754. D/d by sea to Santiago de Cuba and re-assembled in May 1977. Transferred to Aero Caribbean in 1995.

CU-T1214: An-24RV c/n 9404. D/d 1974. Turbojet-boosted export version, similar to the An-24V but fitted with a 1,985lb (8830N) thrust auxiliary turbojet engine in the starboard nacelle. Originally supplied to the Cuban A/F as CU-T923. Transferred to Cubana in Jun 2008, then to Aerogaviota in 2011. In May 2021, it was reported that the aircraft, while on a major check at Baracoa airport, was transferred to Cuban customs for training purposes. It was seen in May 2021 being towed through the streets of Havana in an all-turquoise c/s with a yellow cheatline, nose and engine nacelle.

CU-T1215: IL-62M c/n 8243. D/d Feb 1978. Last flight 31 Jul 1995. Last seen Havana Jul 1999 wfu. Not in the 2001 fleet list. B/u.

CU-T1216: IL-62M c/n 9748. D/d Jun 1978. Wfu Nov 1996; not in 1998 fleet list. B/u.

Another hangar scene at Santa Fé. (Jan Kopp)

A very Cuban scene, as an An-2 sits outside the control tower at Santa Fé. (Jan Kopp)

CU-T1217: IL-62M c/n 3232. D/d Jul 1979. Noted Havana Mar 2006 wfu. Not in the 2002 fleet list. B/u.

CU-T1218: IL-62M c/n 5657. D/d May 1980. Seen stored in Havana in Nov 1998; not in 2001 fleet list. B/u.

CU-T1219: Yak-40 c/n 0959. D/d by sea to Santiago de Cuba and re-assembled in May 1979. On 3 Feb 1980, the aircraft was on a scheduled flight to Baracoa when it crashed on landing. The forward fuselage section of a Yak-40 in Cubana c/s was seen at the junction of the approach road to Santiago de Cuba airport in Oct 1989, with this airframe being the most likely candidate as the only Cuban Yak-40 to have been involved in an accident prior to that date. Cfit. W/o.

CU-T1220: Yak-40 c/n 1059. D/d by sea to Santiago de Cuba and re-assembled in May 1979. Seen in Prague in Oct 1990, then with Aero Caribbean in Jan 1991.

CU-T1221: Yak-40 c/n 1159. D/d by sea to Santiago de Cuba and re-assembled May 1979. With Aero Caribbean in Dec 1993; also leased to Oriental A/L in Venezuela as YV-594C, but appears not to have flown after that. Seen in Havana Apr 1998 without engines.

CU-T1222: Tu-154B-2 c/n 80A447. D/d Aug 1980. re-registered as CU-C1222 in Oct 1999. Wfu by 2003. Believed b/u.

CU-T1223: An-24RV c/n 9405. D/d in 1974 to Cuban A/F as CU-T924. Transferred to Cubana in 2008 as CU-T1223, then to Aerogaviota in Apr 2014 as CU-T1463. Believed b/u 2015.

CU-T1224: Tu-154B-2 c/n 81A493. D/d Jul 1981; b/u by 1998. This registration was also briefly carried by an AN-24. See below.

CU-T1224: An-24RV c/n 9405. Built in 1974. Originally CU-T924, then registered as CU-T1224 in 2008. Transferred to Aerogaviota as CU-T1463 in 2014. Wfu.

CU-T1225: IL-62M c/n 9845. D/d Jun 1981. Last flight 17 Jun 2000. Noted in Havana in Apr 2004 being b/u.

CU-T1226: IL-62M c/n 2219. D/d Jul 1982. Wfu Jun 1995; not in the 1998 fleet list. B/u.

CU-T1227: Tu-154B2 c/n 82A541. D/d Jun 1982. Crashed on approach to Mexico City on 14 Sep 1991. The crew aborted the first approach after failing to make visual contact with the runway. Visibility was reduced and poor, although other aircraft were landing. On the second approach, the aircraft strayed from its final approach and remained above the glideslope. The crew had allowed the aircraft to touch down over half the length of the runway but did not want to make a third approach because they were running short of fuel. Touchdown was finally executed on the last third of runway 05R, and the aircraft came to rest after striking an ILS antenna, some 500m from a busy highway that surrounds the airport. W/o.

CU-T1228: An-26 c/n 126-04. D/d 1982. See CU-T1401.

CU-T1230: An-26 c/n 4306. D/d Nov 1985. Originally d/d to Cuban A/F as 14-07, though military use not confirmed. Seen in 1988 painted as CUT-1407, but later corrected to CU-T1407. Seen as CU-T1230 in 2002. Reportedly stored at Ciudad Libertad.

CU-T1231: An-26 c/n 7303. Built in Apr 1979. Originally with Russian A/F as RA-47334, and Cuban A/F as 12-31. Transferred to Cubana as CU-T1231 in Nov 1980, then to Aero Caribbean in Oct 1985 as CU-T112.

CU-T1232: Yak-40K c/n 1060. Combi/cargo version. D/d by sea to Santiago de Cuba and assembled in 1980. Originally operated by the Cuban Air Force. Seen with Cubana c/s in Mar 1989. Transferred to Aero Caribbean in 1990.

CU-T1236: An-24RV c/n 8102. Built Oct 1972. Originally with Aeroflot Central Region as CCCP-46484, then to Kursk State Air Enterprise in 1993 with the same registration. In Jul 2001, it was registered as ER-AWH with Aerocom of Moldova. Transferred to Cubana in Dec 2001. Still in the fleet list by Dec 2005, but stored in Havana by 2007; briefly preserved west of Terminal 3 at the Havana 'Air Park'. Believed b/u.

CU-T1237: An-24RV c/n 8909. Built 1973. Originally with Aeroflot Central Region as CCCP-46641, then re-registered as RA-46641 before being transferred to Kursk State Air Enterprise in 1994. Sold to Ukraine in an unairworthy condition. Received by Cubana in Feb 2002. Reported to be in storage by 2007 and then moved to a Ministry of the Interior training site between Havana and Cruz del Norte for anti-terrorist training. Last seen Feb 2019.

CU-T1238: An-24 c/n 7803 Built Jul 1979. Originally CCCP-47324, then d/d to Cuban A/F the same month as 12-38. Four days later transferred to Cubana as CU-T1238. Transferred to Aerogaviota in Oct 2002. Wfu in 2005.

CU-T1239: An-24 c/n 7907. Built Jul 1979. Originally CCCP-47325, then d/d to Cuban A/F as 12-39. Later transferred to Angolan A/F as T-239 in 1981. Returned to Cuba in Dec 1987 and registered with Cubana as CU-T1239. Transferred to Aerogaviota in 1995. Re-registered as CU-T1417 in 2001. Last heard of in storage at Vilo Acuña Airport.

CU-T1242: Yak-42D c/n 4549. Believed to be first registered in Mar 2003. Returned to Tatarstan Airlines as RA-42380 by Mar 2005.

CU-T1243: Yak-42D c/n 4340. From Aero Asia International based in Karachi as RA-42374; d/d 2001. Returned to Russia 2005. Wfu 2011.

CU-T1244: An-24RV c/n 0301. Built 1975. Originally with MIAT Mongolian Airlines as BNMAU-1030, then re-registered in 2005 as MT-1011, then JU-1011 in 1998 and later stored. Delivered to Cubana in 2004. Wfu.

CU-T1245: IL-62MK c/n 4512. Originally CCCP-86503 with Soviet A/F, then RA-86503 with Dalavia. Leased from Oct 2004 then returned to Dalavia in Feb 2006.

CU-T1246: Yak-42D c/n 1397. D/d Mar 2005. See also CU-T1704.

CU-T1247: Yak-42D c/n 9017. Leased Oct 2005 to Oct 2008 from Avia Karat. Formerly UN-42712 with Air Kazakhstan, then Armavia (Armenia) as EK-42447. Wfu in 2009. B/u.

CU-T1248: IL-62M c/n 0748. Built Feb 1982. Originally CCCP-86493, then RA-86493. Transferred to Cubana Jun 2005 in basic Dalavia c/s with 'Cubana' titles. Returned to Dalavia in Jun 2006. Dalavia's operator's certificate was revoked and the aircraft was stored in Khabarovsk, Russia.

CU-T1249: Yak-42D c/n 6677. Previously RA-42444. Leased Apr 2005 and returned to Russia in Apr 2007, and took up previous registration.

CU-T1250: IL-96-300M c/n 2015. D/d 30 Dec 2005; returned to Voronezh in Sep 2017 for maintenance. Last noted in Mar 2022 and stored in Havana.

CU-T1251: IL96-300 c/n 2016. D/d Mar 2006. Occasionally used as VIP aircraft for Fidel Castro; used for 'hot and high' trials in Ecuador by Ilyushin in Cubana colour scheme after delivery. Stored at Havana by Jan 2020. Returned to service Nov 2020 following a 'C' check. Still flying in early 2022.

CU-T1252: IL-62M c/n 3341 d/d Apr 1983; last flight 28 Apr 1995; wfu by Nov 1986. Not in 1998 fleet list; b/u.

CU-T125:3 Tu-154B-2 c/n 83A576. D/d Jun 1983. Seen derelict in Havana in May 2006. Believed b/u.

CU-T1254: Il-96-300 c/n 2017. D/d Dec 2006. Last known flight Paris Orly – Santiago de Cuba – Havana on 10 Dec 2012. Initially used for spares. Reported in Jan 2019 as being prepared for ferry to Russia using parts from CU-T1717. Test flown 28 Mar 2019 in preparation for return to Russia for overhaul, after which it was reported that more work was required to make it airworthy enough to fly back to Russia; last seen in Havana in Mar 2020. Reg also used for a Cuban A/F aircraft with serial 12-54.

CU-T1255: Yak 42D c/n 6664. D/d Aug 2007. Previously RA-42443. Ferried from Havana to Kazan in Jul 2010.

CU-T1256: Tu-154B-2 c/n 84A599. D/d Jun 1984. Originally CCCP-85599, but cancelled by Aeroflot. Wfu by Mar 2000. Believed b/u.

CU-C1257: An-24RV c/n 9104. Built Nov 1973. Originally with Aeroflot as CCCP-46645, then as RA-46645 to Penza Aviation Enterprise in Mar 1993. Transferred to Aero Caribbean in Jul 2002, first as CU-T1536, then re-registered in Dec 2005 as CU-T1257. To Cubana in Apr 2006 and painted in retro colour scheme in Aug 2009 with registration changed to CU-C 1257. Wfu and operated as a restaurant in Santa Clara.

CU-T1258: IL-76MD c/n 4615. D/d Sep 1984. Re-registered as CU-C1258 in 1996, then CU-C1419. Sent to Moldova as ER-IBE following conversion to a TD. For sale on the internet in Jul 2005 for US$1.7m. Sold to Angola as D2-FCO in Jul 2006. Wfu. B/u by Aug 2015. See also CU-C1419.

This utility version CU-C1026 sits outside in the Cuban sun. (Jan Kopp)

CU-T1259: IL-62M c/n 5111. D/d Jul 1984; Originally CCCP-75562. Last flight 3 Mar 1998. Seen until Jan 2011 on display, in all white c/s with multi-coloured triangles painted on the fuselage and tail, used as bar with 'Bar Cafeteria' titles, but subsequently vandalised and b/u Mar 2011.

CU-T1260: An-24RV c/n 0307. Built 1975. Originally to Aeroflot Central Region as CCCP-47307 and delivered to Cubana Mar 1984. One of three aircraft substantially modified in Cuba to reduce weight and improve fuel consumption, in order to compete with the Fokker 27s. Named *La Pinta* after completion; not in the fleet list for Feb 2002. Last seen Havana in Jan 2011. Wfu.

CU-T1261: An-24RV c/n 8501. Originally CCCP-46515 with Aeroflot Komi and received by Cubana in Dec 1984. Seen regularly until Jul 1999. Not in 2001 fleet list. Likely to be one of two An-24RVs seen in Havana in Apr 2002, in basic ex-Cubana c/s with registrations removed, wfu/derelict, one with the fuselage in two sections.

CU-T1262: An-24RV c/n 7610. D/d Mar 1985. Originally CCCP-47196. Built for Aeroflot Latvia. One of three aircraft (see also CU-T1260 and CU-T1267), substantially modified in Cuba to reduce weight and improve fuel consumption, in order to compete with the Fokker F-27s. Named *La Santa Maria* after completion. As the aircraft departed Santiago de Cuba airport for a scheduled flight to Havana, on 11 Jul 1997, and was climbing through a height of 500ft (152m), it began to bank to the left, reportedly because of a left engine failure. It then began to descend until it crashed into the sea approximately 3 miles (5km) from the airport. The wreckage could not be recovered from the extremely deep Cayman Trough. W/o.

CU-T1263: An-24RV c/n 9610. Built Jul 1974. Originally CCCP-46678, then RA-46678 in Aug 1993. To Penza Air and then sold to Cubana in Sep 2001. Still in the fleet list at end of 2005. Wfu by 2006 and reported in storage in 2007. B/u in Aug 2008.

CU-T1264: Tu-154M c/n 85A720. Reportedly registered as CCCP-85720 but ntu. This serial number coincides with the c/n. D/d Feb 1986. W/o 29 Aug 1998 at Quito, Ecuador. The aircraft was preparing to make the short flight to Guayaquil before continuing to Havana. During the first engine start, a pneumatic valve was blocked. The problem was rectified, and two engines were started with ground power. The third one was started as the aircraft taxied to the runway. After obtaining take-off clearance, the throttles were advanced, and the aircraft accelerated down runway 17. When the aircraft reached Vr (rotate) speed, it would not rotate. It took the crew ten seconds to decide to abort the take-off. With 2625ft (800m) of runway length remaining, brakes were applied. The aircraft overshot the runway and crashed into a football field, barely missing a residential area. It is presumed that because of the problems during start-up and the time, almost 38 minutes, that passed to the beginning of take-off, the final points of the checklist for taxiing were not complied with, and the crew forgot to select the switches for the hydraulic valves of the control system. W/o.

CU-T1265: Tu-154M c/n 87A751. D/d Jul 1987. Stayed in fleet until Dec 1999. Transferred to Russian register as RA-85721 in Oct 2000, then to Bulgaria as LZ-HMS and later to Russia again as RA-85721.

CU-T1266: An-24RV c/n 0107. Built 1975. Operated by Aeroflot Central Region as CCCP-46533 and to Cubana in Feb 1987. Still operational in Mar 2000, but no longer in the fleet by Feb 2002. Likely to be one of two aircraft seen in Havana in Apr 2002 with registrations removed. Wfu.

Showing the typical Empresa Nacional de Servicios Aéreos colour scheme, this An-2 awaits its next mission. (Jan Kopp)

CU-T1267: An-24RV c/n 9907. Built 1974. Operated by Aeroflot Central Region as CCCP-46696. Originally painted as CUT-1267. Named *La Nina*. Delivered to Cuba in Mar 1987. Last seen in Havana in Jan 2011. Wfu.

CU-T1268: IL-18D c/n 0704. D/d Apr 1986. Originally CCCP-74256. Operated by Aero Caribbean 1992, then leased to Taino Airlines, an airline based on the Caribbean island of Dominica, as a sub-lease from Aero Caribbean, then back to Aero Caribbean and re-registered as CU-T1517 in Jan 2001.

CU-T1269: IL-18V c/n 0701. Originally CCCP-75562. Built 1958. Moved around various Aeroflot divisions before del to Cubana in Jun 1987 in full colours but with very small titles. Transferred to Aero Caribbean Jun 1992; b/u 1999.

CU-T1270: IL-18D c/n 0301. Built Sep 1967. D/d May 1987. Fitted with an additional centre-section tank. Originally CCCP-75459. Went to Mali as TZ-ADF Oct 1974. Returned to Aeroflot in Jun 1985, then to Cubana. Went on lease to East West Chile in Feb 1992, then on return transferred to Aero Caribbean in Nov 92. W/o on 15 Nov 1992 near Puerto Plata (Dominican Republic).

CU-T1271: IL-76MD c/n 9767. D/d Mar 1985. Seen in Havana in Mar 2000 stored in faded c/s. Last flight 4 Jan 1997. Was not in fleet list in Feb 2002. Seen in Havana unmarked and without colours, down on its tail, nose up; gone by Jan 2003. B/u.

CU-T1272: Yak-42D c/n 1442. Previously RA-42364 of Volga Airlines. D/d Aug 2001. Ferried to Odesa in Dec 2009. Re-registered as CU-T1709 Oct 2008. To Ukraine in Aug 2012 as UR-CKO. Returned to Cubana in Aug 2010 but was back in Odesa by Jan 2012. See also CU-T1709.

CU-T1273: Yak-42D c/n 4340. D/d May 2001. Originally RA-42374 of Tatarstan Airlines. Returned to Tatarstan in Apr 2004. CU-T1274 Yak-42D c/n 2606204. Previously RA-42335. D/d Sep 2000. Returned to Russia and re-registered as RA-42335 in Aug 2003.

CU-T1274: Yak-42D c/n 6204. Leased in 2000, then returned to Russia for operation by Kazan Air Enterprise as RA-42335 in Aug 2003. B/u Jan 2012.

CU-T1275: Tu-154M c/n 88A777. D/d Jul 1988. Flown to Samara via Shannon in May 2001 and leased to Samara Airlines with Cuban registration but with titles removed. Then became LZ-HMF by Jun 2003. B/u 2015.

CU-T1276: Tu-154M c/n 85A719. Originally 8R-GGA with Guyana Airways in Mar 1986. Transferred to Cubana in Dec 1988 and to Omskavia (AirUnion) in Russia as RA-85818 by Jan 1996.

CU-T1277: Yak-42D c/n 6238. D/d Sep 1990. Seen in Santiago de Cuba Mar 2000. Wfu. Not in the 2001 fleet list. Named *Santiago de Cuba*.

CU-T1278: Yak-42D c/n 6269. D/d Nov 1990. Seen in Aug 2001 en route to Saratov. With LY-SKC of Aurela Lithuania between 2003 and 2004, then South Airlines in Ukraine as UR-CFA, then Marsland Aviation, in Sudan, with the same registration. Returned to Cuba as CU-T1707 in 2010 but stored by 2012. Preserved at Parque de los Sueños, Santiago de Cuba, as a visitor attraction offering virtual flights to Havana by means of ten TV screens in the passenger cabin.

CU-T1279: Yak-42D c/n 4057. D/d Aug 1991; Believed to have been sub-leased from Tatarstan Air. Ferried to Kazan in 2002 and stored without engines. Wfu 2006. c/n reported in official Russian document as ending '14056' rather than '14057'. No longer in the Cubana fleet list by Dec 2005.

CU-T1280: IL-62M c/n 9648. D/d Mar 1988. Named *15 de Febrero*. Ferried to DPRK (North Korea) in Jul 2012 for Air Koryo as P-886P, but b/u in DPRK in 2013 for parts.

CU-T1281: IL-62M c/n 0453. D/d Feb 1989. During a take-off in poor weather (heavy rainfall, low clouds and 30–40kph winds) from Havana on the first leg of a charter flight to Milan on 3 Sep 1989, when it took off in poor weather. After becoming airborne, the aircraft was caught in downdraughts and descended again after having reached a height of 56m; it then struck ILS aerials 67 seconds after commencing the take-off run, and, 220m behind the runway threshold, broke up and burst into flames as it proceeded up a hill before crashing into a residential area. All 11 crew members and 115 passengers were killed, plus 24 persons on the ground. It was believed that the pilot should not have taken off in such rapidly deteriorating weather.

CU-T1282: IL-62M c/n 2436. D/d Sep 1990. Last flight 03 Jul 2004; total hours 20,033 and 4,725 cycles. Seen in Havana in Mar 2007, with engines missing. Photo on the Aviación en Cuba Facebook site shows it being broken up; date given as 10 Mar 2009; only the rear half of the fuselage sitting on its tail survived by then.

CU-T1283: IL-62M c/n 3823. D/d early 1991. Dbr 20 Apr 2008 on a flight between Santo Domingo and Havana, when a failed inter-shaft bearing in No.2 engine led to an uncontained engine failure while the aircraft was climbing through 25,000ft 45nm from Santo Domingo airport. The fuselage was damaged by the loose turbine blades, and a fire erupted due to compromised fuel lines to engine No.1, but the aircraft managed to land safely at Santo Domingo, and all 117 occupants escaped unhurt. The aircraft was provisionally repaired and ferried to Havana, but later determined to be a write-off. Seen in Havana in Aug 2008. The aircraft was subsequently preserved west of Terminal 3 at Havana 'Air Park'; still there until Nov 2011, but b/u shortly afterwards.

CU-T1284: IL-62M c/n 3732. Built Mar 1991. Last flight on 1 Mar 2011. Seen in Havana in Nov 2020. Wfu. Aircraft was earmarked to be preserved, however, the condition of the interior was very poor. B/u Apr 2021.

CU-T1285: Yak 42D c/n 4068. D/d 1991. The aircraft was operating a scheduled flight between Havana and Caracas, Venezuela, on 25 Dec 1999 when it had to divert to Valencia. The aircraft went into a holding pattern for 40 minutes before crashing into San Luis hill, 7.5 miles (12km) from Valencia. The last contact with the aircraft was when the pilot radioed the Valencia control tower to say that he was descending from 8,000 to 4,000ft (2,438 to 1,219m) as part of his approach. Cfit. W/o.

CU-T1294: An-24RV c/n 8105. Built 1972. Originally CCCP-46487 with Aeroflot Latvia, then to Latavio Latviyskie Avialinii as YL-LCF. Registration cancelled in Oct 1992. Delivered to Cubana in May 1996. On 31 Mar 2003, the aircraft, on a flight between Nueva Gerona and Havana, was hijacked by a man who was believed to be carrying two grenades. The aircraft landed at Havana, where it was refuelled, and, following the release of at least 26 passengers, the aircraft departed for Key West, Florida. The aircraft then became the subject of a lawsuit and was sold at auction for US$6,500 to a Matthew Overton, but the new owner did not immediately move it. Seen at airport at Key West Apr 2021. The intention is now to sink the aircraft nearby at Cayo Hueso, as part of an artificial reef.

CU-T1295: An-24RV c/n 7508. Built 1972. Previously CCCP-47691, then re-registered in Oct 1994 as RA-47691 of Stavropol Avia. D/d to Cubana Dec in 1996. W/o at Nueva Gerona on 14 Jun 2003. A lack of fluid in the hydraulic system meant that there was insufficient pressure to lower the landing gear. The gear was extended using the emergency system. Attempts to extend the flaps using the emergency system failed, and the emergency braking system was also inoperative. The aircraft landed at the start of runway 05 and travelled a distance of 1.5 miles (2.5km). It then left the runway and ran onto uneven terrain and finally stopped in an artificial lake. As a result of the movement off the runway over irregular terrain, the front and left landing gear was badly damaged. The aircraft was recovered by two helicopters shortly after the accident. Dbr.

CU-T1298: Yak-40 c/n 1160. See CU-T1448.

CU-T1299: An-24RV c/n 9108. Built 1973. Originally with Aeroflot as CCCP-46648, then Saravia as RA-46648. D/d to Cubana in Jul 2000 and wfu 2006. Last flight Dec 2004 and b/u Jun 2008.

CU-T1401: An-26 c/n 2604. D/d 1982. Initially to A/F as 14-01, then re-registered as CU-T1401 in 1993, then to Aerogaviota in 1996. Modified to a weather control aircraft by Aerogaviota at Havana in Aug 2007. With Cubana in 2002. Seen abandoned at Baracoa in 2020.

CU-C1419: IL-76MD. See also CU-T1258.

The huge radial engine of the An-2 is clearly visible in this photo. (Jan Kopp)

CU-T1420: An-26 c/n 6607. D/d 1978. Originally with Cuban A/F as 12-20, later 14-20, then in 1986 with Cubana as CU-T1420. Transferred to Aerogaviota in 1995. Believed to be b/u.

CU-T1436: An-26 c/n 7406. D/d Apr 1979. Originally CCCP-47337 and initially operated by the Cuban A/F as 12-36, then re-serialled as 14-36. With Cubana by 1987. Overran the runway at Santiago de Cuba airport, whilst on a flight to Havana, following an aborted take-off on 23 Mar 1990. W/o.

CU-T1440: Yak-40 c/n 2149 (may also be 1049). See CU-T1207.

CU-T1441: Yak 40. See CU-T1206.

CU-T1442: Yak-40 c/n 1445. D/d by sea to Santiago de Cuba and re-assembled in May 1977. To Cuban A/F as 12-42 then to Cubana pre-1989. Stored at Playa Baracoa in 2003 and b/u there between 2010 and 2016.

CU-T1443: Yak-40 c/n 0752. D/d by sea to Santiago de Cuba and re-assembled in May 1977. With Cuban A/F as 12-43, then Cubana. Last seen operational at Holguin in Oct 1998. B/u at Ciudad Libertad.

CU-T1448: Yak-40 c/n 1160. D/d by sea to Santiago de Cuba and re-assembled in 1980 for Cuban A/F as FAR 12-48. With Cubana in Mar 1989 as CU-T1448, then with Aerogaviota in May 1995.

Then registered as TG-YAK and delivered to Mayan World Airlines of Guatemala. Then re-registered as CU-T1298, with large 'Mayan' and small 'Aero Caribbean' tiles. Believed to be dbr on landing and wfu.

CU-C1419: IL-76MD c/n 4615. See also CU-T1258.

CU-T1517: IL-18D c/n 0704. D/d 17 Apr 1968. Transferred to Aero Caribbean in Mar 1992. See also CU-T1268.

CU-T1700: Tu-204C(E) c/n 036. Built Aug 1998. First registered as RA-64036. Flown with large 'Cubana Cargo' titles. D/d in Jul 2007. Ceased flying in Nov 2010 and was then stored without engines in 2020.

CU-T1701: Tu-204-100 B/E c/n 035. Built Sep 2006, but version changed during construction and was shown as -120SE. Registered as RA-64035. D/d Dec 2007. Last seen, without engines, in Havana in 2020.

CU-C1702: Tu-204-100 B/E c/n 042. D/d Dec 2007. Noted in Shannon in Jul 2019 en route to Ulyanovsk for overhaul.

CU-C1703: Tu-204-200 c/n 037. D/d Apr 2009. Version changed during construction to Tu-204CE.

CU-T1704: Yak-42D c/n 1397. D/d Mar 2005 as CU-T1246, on lease from Tulpar Air, Russia. Then re-registered as CU-T1704 in 2008 and returned to Russia in Sept 2010. B/u Jan 2014 in Kazan, Russia.

CU-T1705: Yak-42D c/n 4576. Formerly UR-42381 with Donbassaero. D/d Apr 2009 on lease and returned in Jun 2010. Became UR-42381. Later destroyed during separatist fighting at Donbas airport Ukraine in Oct 2014.

CU-T1706: AN-24RV c/n 0701. Built 1976. First registered in 1977 as RDPL-34007 with Lao Airlines, then with Lao People's Liberation Army Air Force in 1994. Then re-registered as RDPL-34151 to Lao Capricorn Air 2006. Seen in Kyiv in May 2009, with all-white c/s and marked '10701'. For sale on internet in mid-2009, priced at US$930,000 with just 2,200 hours in the logbook. Departed Kyiv in Dec 2009 using Cubana callsign. Performed Cubana's last An-24 flight in Dec 2012, then transferred to Aerogaviota as CU-T1464 in Dec 2018. Reported as stored Dec 2020.

CU-T1707: Yak-42D c/n 6235. Delivered Feb 2010. Put into storage 2012, then ferried to Odesa in Nov 2012, to be registered as UR-CFH. Cuban registration cancelled Jun 2013.

CU-T1708: See CU-T1278.

CU-T1709: See CU-T1272.

CU-T1710: An-158 c/n 201-01. The first production An-158. D/d Apr 2013. Damaged when a fire extinguisher exploded in the cabin; maintenance started Aug 2014, but not completed as of Apr 2017.

CU-T1711: An-158 c/n 201-02. Carried only '32' during initial production in 2013. D/d Jul 2013. Believed to be grounded owing to its unsatisfactory technical condition and a lack of spares.

CU-T1712: An-158 c/n 201-03. Originally registered as UR-EXC. D/d Oct 2013. Grounded in Apr 2016 owing to a damaged door.

CU-T1714: An-158 c/n 201-04. D/d May 2014. The only Cubana An-158 still in service by late 2017.

CU-T1715: An-158 c/n 201-05. D/d Aug 2014. Grounded owing to its operational condition and a lack of spares. Operational again by Sep 2017. Last seen in Havana in Apr 2019.

CU-T1716: An-158 c/n 205-06 (note change of c/n prefix). D/d Jun 2015. Last revenue flight Apr 2017. Grounded owing to its unsatisfactory technical condition and a lack of spares. Noted flying between Havana and Santiago de Cuba in Feb 2018.

CU-T1717: IL-96-300 c/n 1005. Built in Jul 1993 as RA-96008 and served with Aeroflot between mid-1993 and Mar 2014, the last IL-96 to do so. D/d 31 Aug 2014. Leased from Ilyushin Finance. Initially in basic Aeroflot c/s with 'Cubana' titles; tail repainted in Cubana colours, but the fuselage remained in basic Aeroflot c/s and still carried the name *I. Moiseyev* after Igor Moiseyev, a famous Ukrainian-born choreographer who lived to be 101. Nicknamed 'Juana Bacallao' after a Cuban singer and musician, who at the time of writing is 97, but the name is not painted on. Parts from it used to repair CU-T1254, in Jan 2019, enabling it to fly to Russia for maintenance.

CU-TXXX: (unallocated) IL-96-300 c/n 1008. D/d to Aeroflot in Oct 1994 as RA-96011. The intention was for the aircraft to be transferred to Cubana in 2014, but a dispute with the leasing company meant that the aircraft was never delivered.

Leased Aircraft

The following aircraft were supplied to Cubana on leases. There is a total of 26 IL-62s, many of which were on short-term leases, but continued to carry their Soviet registrations. The aircraft also retained their Aeroflot colour scheme, often with a small Cubana sticker.

CCCP-85223: Tu-154B-1 c/n 77A223. Leased to Cubana between Aug and Nov 1979.

CCCP-85400: Tu-154B-2 c/n 80A400. Leased direct from the factory between 1980 and 1981, then transferred to Aeroflot's Donavia division.

CCCP-86605: IL-62 c/n 41701. D/d on lease from Nov 1974 until May 1977.

CCCP-86606: IL-62 c/n 41702. D/d on lease from Jan 1975 until Sep 1975.

CCCP-86607: IL-62M c/n 41703. D/d on lease from Mar 1976 until Aug 1978.

CCCP-86608: IL-62 c/n 41704. D/d on lease from Dec 1974 until Jul 1977.

CCCP-86610: IL-62 c/n 41801. D/d on lease from Jan 1975 until Dec 1977.

CCCP-86618: IL-62M c/n 20422. On lease between Nov 1975 and Feb 1976.

CCCP-86621: IL-62M c/n 20556. On lease between Dec 1975 and Feb 1976.

CCCP-86649: IL-62 c/n 00703. Built Jul 1970. D/d on lease during 1976.

CCCP-88650: IL-62M c/n 00705. D/d on lease from Jan 1973 until May 1973. D/d to Aeroflot in Aug 1970, then to EgyptAir as SU-ARO, then reverted to CCCP-88650 before lease to Cubana. Eventually returned to Ulyanovsk.

CCCP-86652: IL-62 c/n 00802. D/d on lease from Feb to Oct 1974. Built and d/d to Aeroflot in 1970. Briefly carried KLM markings, then to EgyptAir SU-AVU, then reverted to CCCP-86652 prior to lease to Cubana.*

CCCP-86654: IL-62 c/n 00804. Built and d/d to Aeroflot in 1971. Leased to KLM between Oct 1971 and Jun 1972, then became SU-AVL with EgyptAir, before reverting to CCCP-86654 prior to lease to Cubana between Dec 1972 and Aug 1974.*

CCCP-86655: IL-62 c/n 00805. Built and d/d to Aeroflot in 1971. Leased to KLM between Apr 1971 and Oct 1972, then became SU-AVW with EgyptAir, before reverting to CCCP-86655 prior to lease to Cubana from Nov 1973 until May 1976.*

CCCP-86656: IL-62M c/n 00901. Built 1967. Leased 1974–1975.

CCCP-86672: IL-62 c/n 70302. Built Jun 1968. D/d on lease May 1974 and stayed in the fleet until 1983.

CCCP-86677: IL-62 c/n 80402. Built Oct 1968. D/d on lease between Dec 1973 and Mar 1976.

CCCP-86681: IL-62 c/n 90501. Built Feb 1969. D/d on lease between Jul 1973 and Jul 1974.

CCCP-86685: IL-62 c/n 90505. Built Sep 1969. D/d on lease between May and Sep 1973.

CCCP-86686: IL-62 c/n 90601. Built Oct 1969. D/d on lease Apr 1973 to Jun 1974.

CCCP-86687: IL-62 c/n 90604. Built Jan 1970. D/d on lease from Apr 1973 until Jun 1973.

CCCP-86689: IL-62 c/n 11001. Built Aug 1971. D/d on lease from Sep 1972 to Aug 1974. The aircraft was allocated the registration CU-T994, but it appears not to have been used.

CCCP-86690: IL-62 c/n 11002. Built and delivered to Aeroflot in 1971. Leased to KLM then to Cubana between Sep 1972 and Apr 1973 and briefly again in May 1973.*

CCCP-86691: IL-62 c/n 11003. Built and d/d to Aeroflot in 1971. Leased to Cubana between Nov 1972 and Feb 1976.

CCCP-86694: IL-62 c/n 11104. Built Mar 1972. D/d in Jan 1974 on lease from Sep 1975 until Jan 1977.

CCCP-86697: IL-62 c/n 21301. Built Oct 1972. D/d in Feb 1974 on lease until Jun 1975.

CCCP-86704: IL-62 c/n 41603. Built Mar 1974. D/d Sep 1974 on lease until Feb 1977.

CCCP-86705: IL-62M c/n 41605. Built May 1974. D/d in Mar 1976 on lease until 1977.

YR-IMG: IL-18 c/n 7301. Leased from Tarom between 1989 and 1990, then became ER-ICG with Renan Airlines of Moldova.

YR-IRC: IL-62 c/n 1902. Leased from Tarom. D/d in Jan 1990 and returned to Tarom in Nov 1990.

YR-IRE: IL-62M c/n 1628. Leased from Tarom between Nov 1989 and Aug 1990.

* While not directly linked to Cubana, the background to this unusual move is interesting. In 1971, KLM agreed a joint venture with Aeroflot, enabling them to fly from Amsterdam via Moscow to Tokyo over Russia, taking the Trans-Siberian route, one that was previously forbidden. The flight was operated once a week by an Aeroflot flight deck and a KLM cabin crew, and the routing allowed four hours to be cut from the normal flight time. The first flight took place on 6 Apr 1971 with CCCP-86652. The arrangement lasted until 31 Oct 1972, but it was 1987 before KLM was given permission to use the route again in its own right.

Bibliography

Detailed information on Soviet-built airliners courtesy of:
https://www.airhistory.net/info/soviet.php
http://rzjets.net/aircraft/
https://www.facebook.com-aviación en cuba
https://russianplanes.net/ (in Russian)
www.oldjets.net

Tu-154B-2 CU-T1256 takes a break between flights at Varadero in this 1997 photo. (Damiano Gualdoni via urrib2000)

Other books you might like:

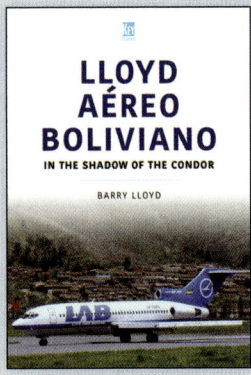

Airlines Series,
Vol. 8

Airlines Series,
Vol. 6

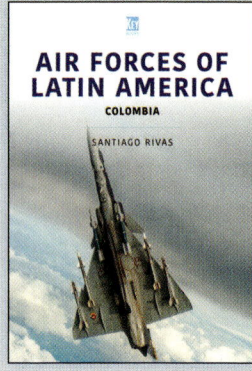

Air Forces Series,
Vol. 5

Modern Military Aircraft
Series, Vol. 2

Airlines Series,
Vol. 9

Historical Commercial
Aircraft Series, Vol. 1

For our full range of titles please visit:
shop.keypublishing.com/books